# praise for *Underwater*

"In *Underwater Daughter*, Antonia Deignan delivers a heart-shattering memoir of painful truth and soulful healing. Word by word, her powerful story dances across the page with lyrical rhythm, all while diving deep into the mind-warping currents of childhood sexual abuse. Readers follow along as she swims through many decades of emotional waves before finally learning to untangle herself from the deep. By the end, we all heal alongside her as she resurfaces to claim the light. A must-read for anyone who has ever suffered abuse at the hands of someone they love—or loved someone who has."

—JULIE CANTRELL, *New York Times* and *USA Today* best-selling author of *Perennials*

"From these pieces emerge a partial sense of how Deignan learned to reconfigure the impact of her physical and psychic pains to achieve healing and forgiveness. *Underwater Daughter* is a poetic memoir about transformation and transcendence after abuse."

—FOREWORD CLARION REVIEWS

"*Underwater Daughter* is pure magic. From her first line to her last, Antonia Deignan takes us on a wild ride, from her perilous childhood through many hardships to the resilient woman she became. Her voice is utterly inventive. Written with stunning originality and passion, this is a book readers will long remember."

—LINDA SCHREYER, television/screenwriter and coauthor of *Tears and Tequila*

"Like the author's dancing, this memoir seems to have some nameless tune in its core. Deignan gently paints a picture of even the most difficult moments in her life. She has decided to live her life lovingly, and in doing so has given us all a path forward."
—HARRIET ROSS, cofounder of Dance for Life and retired general manager of the Joffrey Ballet

"In *Underwater Daughter*, the author bravely faces her humanity and dives into excavating her inner and outer life. Written with a clever hand, the read is intimate and raw, and shares unfiltered vivid memories of abuse, survival, love, trauma, dance, relationships, healing, evolution, and so much more. This memoir is a meaty, meaningful journey that kept me captivated and wanting more."
—SHERRY ZUNKER, founder and creator of BeMoved Dance

"Antonia Deignan makes 'raw' feel very accessible. Her unflinching detail mocks the painful absurdity of a world where brutal adults leave a child holding self-blame in tiny hands. Prepare your senses to move fluidly through her stunning observations, in which she masterfully captures the burden of trauma at a cellular level. Never mind a life of clenched fists and secrets kept; this selfless writer opens her soul so that others may bathe in the bravery of her words. And dance. And heal."
—PAMELA WEISS, founder of Hold This While IP Productions, writer, and producer

"Poetic, descriptive, and segues into scene after scene like a dance . . . vulnerable, raw, and soothing. . . . This took my breath away. I felt this."
—STEPHANIE ARNOLD, producer, speaker, and author of *37 Seconds*

"Antonia Deignan's *Underwater Daughter* is a spellbinding memoir. At once a lyrical portrait of a young woman's coming-of-age and of a mother's coming into herself, it is a beautiful, gripping memoir of love and art, and of overcoming damage through both. *Underwater Daughter* is an odyssey of coming home to oneself by laying claim to one's body and desires—as a dancer, lover, mother, teacher. Wise, moving, instructive, gorgeous."
—E. J. LEVY, author of *The Cape Doctor*

"*Underwater Daughter* starts with disjointed pieces of prose and poetry violently breaking across the page like smashed glass. As you compulsively turn its pages, the writing gradually becomes more lyrical and coherent, the jagged shards subtly glued together to produce a beautiful and colorful mosaic out of all the broken bits. It is a writing style that perfectly suits its underlying subject. This is the story of an abused child, running from her terrors as an adult, finally made whole through self-reflection and a searing honesty. A brave, moving, and compelling work."
—RICHARD C. MORAIS, author of *The Hundred-Foot Journey*

"In a sea of trauma memoirs, Antonia Deignan's *Underwater Daughter* breaks poetically through the surface like sunlight dancing on turbulent water. The evocative and beautifully crafted prose and poems that narrate Deignan's transcendence leap across the pages—the writing has the rhythm that only a trained dancer could produce. Artful, inspiring, and redemptive, *Underwater Daughter* is a book I will turn to again, laced as it is with love, wisdom, art, culture, and the kind of transformational forgiveness and nurturing that is the best of humanity."
—REBECCA BLOOM, founder of Communications Bloom and coauthor of *The Anti-Cookbook*

"In *Underwater Daughter*, Deignan invites the reader to take a deep soul-dive using poetic imagery and beautiful prose to understand the extent of her pain from childhood trauma. Then the author continues her narrative by offering her wisdom regarding the healing power of movement through human suffering, bringing us to the surface again to breathe, heal, dance, and live fully. This book is a beautiful conversation seeking to connect our stories and shift us to greater love. Beautifully done."

—MEG NOCERO, author of *The Magical Guide to Bliss, Sparkle & Shine*, and *Butterfly Awakens: A Memoir of Transformation through Grief*

*Underwater Daughter*

# Underwater Daughter

*A Memoir of Survival and Healing*

Antonia Deignan

SHE WRITES PRESS

Published 2023
Printed in the United States of America
Print ISBN: 978-1-64742-422-0
E-ISBN: 978-1-64742-423-7
Library of Congress Control Number: 2022913366

For information, address:
She Writes Press
1569 Solano Ave #546
Berkeley, CA 94707

Interior Design by Tabitha Lahr

She Writes Press is a division of SparkPoint Studio, LLC.

*for mama*

*"Our own lives are the instruments
with which we experiment with the truth."*
—THICH NHAT HANH

*"Man is the sum of his memories—
if they are gone, who am I?"*
—BARBARA PYLE

a chunky episodic self-selection of memory
a moment-to-moment recall of survival through perception
*controlled hallucination*

# contents

# dream one

*Once upon the waves of a great sea stood a very large iron-framed bed. It was mine. The sea was active and infinite underneath. Peaceful atop the mattress and sensitive to the wisdom beneath me, I mused, "Welcome squid and giant octopi, ancient turtles and fleeing krill chased by mighty whales, rafting shearwaters above rockfish and sardines and squid. Miles of waves in blues laid over fantasia.*

*"We need you," the world of water sang to me, "as much as you need me," the tune went.*

*And the sun continued to light and scramble the silver-blue puzzles underneath my bed. There were ocean's busy lives slipping in and out of safe huddles of grass clusters, slipping from coral skeletons, tricking predators as they quickly hunted for meals, just like me. Before I discovered the mattress on the sea, I didn't know where to hide or find protection when danger came too close, when trespassers stayed. But on the open blue sanctuary, when his hands washed over me, I dove and dipped down, dodged and darted away and died for a while. And when pleasure bubbled inside, because of him, and when dying wasn't enough, I kissed the snake instead, uniting death and the peace of eternal life. I didn't know, until I did, dressed in seaweed's blankets and snakeskin, I was saved.*

*The flying fish flipped and flew, ducking dating dolphins, their whirling, cackling pods in parade; everyone was hungry. We all certainly understood it was fear, the fish and I, eye to eye, swim or die.*

*Luring seagulls to the bedposts, I knot-tied hundreds of their rubbery webbed feet to the iron poles, and as I set their bodies free, we sailed, we flew, we rose blimp-like toward the heavens.*

*My parents weren't invited to my floating bed, but I did, however, parade my joy, and in front of them too, knowing we were all of us just a breath away from predators' appetites anyway.*

*I was the snake head and the tail, the beauty within.*

# part one

## AROUSAL

I was not smart.
I was not educated.
I was not a good partner.
I was not popular.
I was not a good daughter.
I was not a good sister.
I was not a good friend.
I will tell you, look you in the eye, not away like a liar but look you hard in the eye, without a blink, and say I am actually some of those things. But I lie.
I was not athletic.
I was not well-read.
I was not educated.
I was not likable.
I was not pretty.
I was not young.
I was not a good mother.
I was not spiritual.
I was not religious.
I was not trustworthy.
I was not political.
I was not nostalgic.

I was not nuanced.
I was not deep.
I was not flexible.
I was not reliable.
I was not healthy.
I was not sober.
I was not fair.
I was not generous.
I was not truthful.
I was not loved.
I was not a team player.
I was not proud.
I was not natural.
I was not in touch.
I was not a crybaby.
I was not emotional.
I was not prone to outbursts.
I was not horny.
I was not sexy; last two, both lies.
I was not a rapist.
Nor was I a serial killer.
I was not a river.
Nor a tree.
Not a mushroom.
Not the rain.
I was not a hot-air balloon.
I was not a natural swimmer, but with fierce determination
I became one.
I was not a child.
I was not a god.
Help me.

A lounge lizard lived in my home, posing as my brilliant and fumbly dumbly father. I was four when he touched and tickled and weirdly lingered where he shouldn't have in between, at the tip-tops of my pinchable thighs, sweet spots. And I was four when my mother watched him touch and tickle me there. I was four when I played with stuffed toys and wore plastic rings on my fingers. I was four when his touch made me goose-bumpy and squirm in pleasure, innocently. I was four when I found it hard to sit still, ants in my pants, spiraling energy deep within me. At night when my sisters' and brother's noses were tucked into their books in their bedrooms, I tidied my things before bedtime. I waited for him, bubbles inside me. I knew he'd likely come in and make my bubbles bigger. "Go to your room and read," my mother would say, spying me at the door of their bedroom.

My father devoured books. Thrillers, biographies, medical journals, cookbooks, horticulture guides, wine catalogs—all piled high on his desk and on the bookshelves behind him, near his pillow on his bed, ledged at his bed. He read classical music and played it from memory. He had perfect pitch. "What is perfect pitch?" I'd asked my mother.

"Pick a note on the piano," she replied, "he'll tell you what it is and won't watch you choose." When I was four, I realized of course, my dad was magic. He was exceptionally good at all sorts of things. By the time I reached the age of eight, I was masturbating obsessively, smelling and tasting my tanged and honeyed fingertips, riding the waves of his classical music, my interiority, my biology.

My father, hunched and serious, sat at his Steinway building crescendo. He pounded masterpieces into the plush velvet chairs in the far corner of the room; he aroused the floorboards and me below them. Beethoven, Mahler, Rachmaninoff thrilled faster and faster, ripping currents into our family's den, into the soul of the shag carpeting. Symphonic inhales, pleasured exhales in his controlled hands. Perhaps his passion for his music was a cry for help, a silent enemy from his childhood, a perpetrator now held within the divinity of his masterpieces, his fingertips.

My father was rigorously educated, tutored young, and Ivy League polished. "He was such a nice boy, the sweetest boy," his cousin told me once. "He was pushed so hard by his mother with that piano, but he was brilliant, soloing with that orchestra when he was eight," she said, and then again. "He was brilliant."

"C'mon, play a note," my mother coaxed me, poking my shoulder. "He won't look, and he'll tell you what note you played. He's a magician."

My mother was smart and sophisticated and artistic. She had stacks of *New Yorkers* and the *New York Times* flourishing at her bedside. She collected *National Geographic* magazines with their bright yellow covers and splashy sea creatures jumping from its pages—feathered lionfish, see-through anemones, dolphins, clown fish, whales' eyes like galaxy planets. My mother had also studied the piano, but what she truly loved was the ballet. As a teenager, she pored over dance journals, idolized Balanchine and Nureyev, worshipped the famous prima ballerinas, Alicia Markova, Margot Fonteyn, and the blind Alicia Alonso. Consequently, my sisters and I were made to study ballet from the beginning of time.

I attended nursery school at the reform synagogue Temple
Israel. My grandmother was a celebrity of sorts there because
her husband, Poppy, was such a successful local business
owner. Bub volunteered her time and energy in women's
Jewish organizations, often hosting ladies in her home where
they stood in the hallway dressed in knee-length floral-print
dresses and wore dainty and slim-heeled shoes to match.
They smoked cigarettes and ate little sandwiches while seated
at her formal dining table; cold coffee in white cups on sau-
cers, crystal glasses with neat cream sherry. They would all
have been young mothers during the Second World War,
likely praying at night the blessing of being American, likely
praying for someone overseas, a cousin, an uncle, a missing
relative. After my mother celebrated her confirmation, her
reaffirmation to Judaism, she left Temple Israel for good—
that is, until her father died in 1964. And then once more
after that, to honor Bubby's long life, forty years later.

"Who will help me pass out our nap mats?" my nursery teacher, Miss Fennel, sang. She was slender, with wildly
teased, chin-length hair and beautiful white, wide teeth. She
wore mock turtlenecks and slim, pocketless plaid pants over
lace-topped white socks. She was patient. My friend Zoe and

I lay next to one another on the floor during naptime. I gazed at Zoe's wild black curls and pale white skin with dark red smeary lips. She was slim and also wide-eyed with a small, flat nose and asked me often to lick the color off her lips. "Please stay quiet," Miss Fennel sweetly hushed us. "God's listening," I thought I heard her say. I loved naptime during nursery school, curling up and barely touching Zoe's knit sweater, studying the small scoop at her low back, the tip of her tail. Echoing her moon shape while staying within the boundaries of my yellow nap mat, inside me, between my legs, I felt Daddy's tickle. But I never believed God was listening, as Miss Fennel liked to say, because I was certain about where God actually was. God was watering the plants at my house and sitting at her desk and shopping and wiping down the dog's bowl in our kitchen sink; in fact, God once made me eat canned dog food after I told her it would taste better than the dinner she had placed before me, something like lima beans and meat that was smooth and soft like a pillow. I ate dog food.

The actual word *God* was not spoken in my home, and the concept of God rattled me because I was thoroughly convinced God. Was. My. Mother. Full. Stop. (Consequently, God was the one watching my father padiddle me.)

Confirmation pictures lined the walls in the downstairs hallway outside the nursery school room. The women in the photographs wore long white robes, each of them sporting large flowers pinned into their hairdos, an exotic hibiscus, a wild celebration. The young men statued themselves in rows behind the women; their suits were dark, their lips caught parted, secure over demure. There in that photographed milestone, my mother angled inward, her perfect skin and dark hair, one shoulder a tick more forward than the other, leaning toward the camera lens with her knock 'em sock 'em breasts; the silky robe delightfully accentuated her curves, her rubied lips painted coquettishly, her breath hinted at, a warm whisper. The same exact photo hung in Bubby's bedroom and at home in my house, in the hallway.

Bubby wore her dark woolen dress suits at temple, small-heeled black leather shoes with buckles. And her hair was neatly bunned. "Tooner-Pooner," she wooed me while standing next to her friends in the sanctuary; she pulled my tiny body close to hers—gift wrapped me in.

Was it the second or third day after she died, in that same small adjunct sanctuary forty years later, that I prayed at her spot, in her place, and re-memorized her, ghost danced and davened with her? I remembered back to when her feet flatly balanced on those sturdy half-inch heels, how she lovingly gestured her age-spotted hands and lifted veins, how she good-naturedly gripped her siddur. I reimagined her silver drop earrings pivoting my eyes up and toward her as she nodded and laughed, and they swung as she gossiped with the clergy or the cantor. I whiffed her faint mothball smell mixed with sweet talcum powder; the edges of her wool skirt scratched my cheek. *Kiss me, Bub, kiss me.*

I remembered sleepovers at Bub's on Fridays, when sometimes my blue-hued friend Molly who lived next door slept over too. (Molly had a hole in her heart, which resulted in Molly's pleasantly peaceful blueness.) Bub lit the candles and chanted the blessings for Shabbat, still dressed in her temple wool. I stood at Bubby's right side and Molly stood at mine. Bub's horn-rimmed frames slid below the midway point of her nose as she tipped her head forward toward the wicks and light. Molly and I inched closer to Bub's flame. But her dark stockings that latched at her mid-thigh caught my attention, and I was embarrassed. And the garter peeked of course, and her thick calves grew less femininely out of her practical leather shoes. *Come closer*, she must have thought, and her breath bridged me over, linked me into the prayers she chanted, and I watched her create more space with her expanding body and her extending arms, as though it was now that time to include her parents, her ancestors. She was my sanctuary. "*Baruch atah Adonai*," she sang like the Friday before. "*Eloheinu, Melech haolam*," she chanted firmly. "*Asher kid'shanu, b'mitzvotav v'tzivanu, l'hadlik ner shel . . .*" she continued, shaking the lit match until it was out. "Blessed are you, Adonai our God, Sovereign of all, who hallows us with mitzvot, commanding us to kindle the light of Shabbat." We sipped our tiny goblets of Manischewitz wine, "*borei p'ri hagafen*," and made puckery kisses with our lips as we finished all of its sweet liquid darkness. We giggled. My eyes returned to Bub's veined hands and I copied her, tried shaping my mouth to match hers. When she slowly set down the kiddush cup, she finished with "Amen," and the word landed softly on my tongue.

Molly and I would play hide-and-seek after blessings. I'd hide in Bub's bedroom closet, and in the dark I opened the plastic storage drawers stacked under her clothes. I touched the black ribbons I'd seen on Bubby's legs, now in a tangled heap, the garters and belts and flat wired fastens, some ivory-colored ones. Flags of intricately laced belts dropped between my fingers; they smelled of moss and wet soil and teacups and death. I touched my fingertips to my lips and tasted their salt, slowed down my breath. I set a ribbony strap crosswise on the top of my thigh, which flared the desire I still had no name for, my slippery secret. Sudden nearby footfalls and slamming doors switched up my attention, and I quickly returned her intimates and delicate bits to their drawers. I was sticky. Whispers rushed in with the light cracking under the door.

There were also Poppy's *Playboy* magazines stacked high on a shelf inside Bub's closet. Some days I would pull them down and lock myself in her bathroom to read. Columns of stories filled with words I'd not heard of or read before filled its pages. There were cartoons with anatomy parts triple the size of normal: men with comical noses, side-combed hair over thumbprint heads, stick figures underneath except for the mammoth-sized rocket cocks blasting out of undone khakis; lurking behind them were the dark-haired bitches with salami meats launching from their chests. The men cursed like sailors; the women opened up like fish. Photographs. Beautifully curved mermaids, topless, bottomless, women curled and slanted, shirts unbuttoned for the tease, pouting lips wet, glistening eyes shotgun. A centerfold. Pointy hips on the left and right, a waistline you could wear as a bracelet; I flipped and folded, flipped and folded.

I knew Poppy, my grandfather, only because of the photographs Bub had of him on the walls. A handsome Russian immigrant, he died of heart disease a year after I was born. His suits and fedoras and fisherman's caps, his magazines and violins and accomplishments remained silent and tucked away, like the unfathomable Holocaust, like passion and secrets, everything hushed and hidden. Only the sepia-toned photographs fleshed him out in every room of their Tudor home, the squidly ink of him and the generations before him, unsmiling.

Bub had a grand and formal staircase centering the front hall of her home, a favored destination during my child's play and where my mother also lingered and played. The dark wood was partially covered with a Persian runner. A black iron banister beckoned my small hands, just as it had my mother's small hands before mine. The landing overlooked the parkway her home was built along, and one of her many crystal chandeliers hovered within the ascending spiral, alighting more somber relatives dusted and framed on the walls.

In the mornings I watched Bub eat her scrambled eggs and raspberry jam, prepared by Mrs. Walta. "Try it, Tooner," she said, barely sipping her black coffee, settling the clink of the cup into its saucer, never refusing Mrs. Walta's offer of a refill. "Mix the raspberry with the egg," she instructed (which I've done ever since). I loved her chipmunk-chewing, nose-wrinkling mawing of her food, her dry-lined mouth (which I've inherited), her puckered lips sharpening and softening as her teeth chewed and groaned. My mother said eggs and jam was artless.

Mrs. Walta brought us sticky prunes. Bubby ate the hard and dry ones I discarded. "Yes, please," she harrumphed and winked, smuckering stickiness into her kiss, and kneading the sweet paste with her chomping teeth. I pressed the softer ones between my thumb and fingers, squeezed out the pulp, and sucked them down. "Go and get a pop from the cellar," Bub suggested, and I ran to the root cellar's steps toward the basement. The door cricked open and snapped back fast on its hinge as I grabbed the bare bulb's chain and quickly lit the cellar's pantry. Stacked in rows along the lowest shelf sat small bottled six-packs of Coca-Cola, 7Up, and orange Fanta; eight-ounce, glass-paneled bottles with red-cheeked Santas smiling from their widest parts. I barely heard my sister calling me from upstairs, "Bring me and Bub a cream soda, please?"

The tiny bathroom off her kitchen was my favorite bathroom in the house. Down the breakfast nook's bitty steps to the right placed me at its door. On the left was the toilet and straight ahead a second door opposite the one I stood in, which led out and into her library room. There was a freestanding porcelain sink wedged in next to the toilet and a shelf bolted into the wall next to the sink with a bare light bulb in a ceramic base. A twisting knob turned the light bulb on and sounded a hard and satisfying click when I turned it off. *Click. Click.* It was why that bathroom was my favorite. The click.

Through the bathroom window opposite that toilet was a long rocking lounger that sat on the back porch. It swung locomotive-style, front to back, and many nights when I slept in it, the lake winds from across the street breezed through the screened porch walls, calm and dreamy, sometimes moist like an innocent child who had been touched.

Other nights, Bub allowed me to sleep on the chaise lounge near her bed, on its brocaded cushion pillows and musky damask cover. She read every night in her bed, on the far side away from me. Her red velvet bedspread crinkled when she switched the light off, and her little snores percolated quickly after "Good night, Tooner Pooner." "*A gute neshome*," she had whispered.

"Good night, Bub," I whispered back, eyeing the moon through the window. I loved when she told me I was a good soul. *A gute neshome*.

I gravitated toward the licorice she kept in glass jars on the kitchen counter—black licorice spinning wheels and hand-cut red Twizzler sticks. Cheetos and pretzels filled more jars next to the candy; it was a midway of edible delights. In the living room, she filled her lidded silver candy dish with Brach's milky chocolate stars. "Bub?" I'd call out to gauge her whereabouts, the lid hovering over the candy dish in one of my hands. I relied on permission by omission and stuffed them in my mouth, let them slowly melt in the middle of my tongue and above it along my soft palate.

I conjured story lines in her living room and ruled over the invisible family members and other guests I'd invited, sweeping them toward the stuffed Queen Anne chairs with, "Won't you sit here, dear lady." The many framed ancestors and I exchanged pleasantries. I settled them in their places and pointed out to them the Bubela, the guest of honor performing on the grand piano. Applause, applause. I sat beside her, turning the pages of her sheet music; I followed her blue-veined hands, her dancing arthritic fingers. She sat bolt upright and swayed slightly as she played. Mrs. Walta made cucumber and cream cheese tea sandwiches, which I passed out before offering the guests the silver dish of chocolate stars. Bubby never asked me how many of the chocolates I'd eaten or if it was me who emptied the licorice jar. I wasn't sure she noticed, because it was Mrs. Walta who kept charge of those things, refilled them. Maybe Bub never noticed much underneath her royally sloped nose, like my mother said. But it didn't matter to me what she never noticed. What Bub did do was give me permission to freelance amongst her things, to touch and hold them, to open doors and drawers and closets and magazines to see what was hidden inside.

In the large wooden bowl in her library where she read her newspapers sat an assortment of nuts—walnuts, Brazil nuts, almonds, filberts, and pecans. Brass nut crackers lay near the bowl on the table, and with their carved jester's heads and mouths wide open, they mashed and moshed the hard shells into clowned nut meat. Walnuts were bitter and cashews were sweet. "Live every day of your life and love every day you live," Bubby instructed as she bit into a walnut, her old feathery lips quivering.

Later in life, I sat beside my own children when attending services and pressed Hebrew words out of the pages of the prayer book and into my mouth as best I could, assured of Bubby's blessings. My children didn't love Sunday school or learning Hebrew, but it was quickly revealed to them I was not the final stop, the one with all the answers or all the truth. Their studies not only offered the possibility of the mystery of faith but a bounty of information and interpretations of thought way beyond what I had to offer.

I learned the trope of Torah and Haftarah, fell in love with its guttural, soulful patterns. In my forties I became a bat mitzvah, a Jewish adult, with all five of my children, my husband, and my parents there to witness the grandeur, the holier substance of my being manifesting, because of Bubby.

I never went back to Temple Israel or saw Zoe again after nursery school because we moved away to a modernly built, shaggy-floored, triple-decked tower of a home, a fidgety widget rocket ship a suburb away from Minneapolis and Bubby's influence. My bedroom was an open door, and across the hall from their open door, his open door, his side of the bed—his lie the point *b* across from where my head lay on its pillow, point *a*. I slept tickly, where my hands underneath my thin cotton underwear stayed, two fingers from each meeting quietly in the middle, to circle and rise up and down. *G'night, Daddy.*

I filled my empty hours at my mother's house outdoors.
Four years old, I had bangs, blunt and dark. My culottes fell
shy of the middle of my thighs. The polyester material didn't
pick up grass stains, but my shins and ankles and toes did.
I picked the blades of grass off my shorts and rubbed away
the telltale green grass-inked spots on my legs so that my
wandering about outside wouldn't be found out. Between
my teeth I clipped the sweet white-ended tips of the grass
and ate the blades' sugary ends. My hands fisted weeds,
alive and dead. I breathed in the dandelion fluff. I breathed
dandelion yellows and smashed their heads up my nostrils,
short snort-sneezed them back out again, curled them into
my chin like melted butter.

I sat.
drifted.
pretended
I was someone else.

It is a coping mechanism, dissociation. It's the ability to disconnect from your own thoughts, feelings, or sense of self. In science, molecules do the same thing by splitting off and becoming smaller, separate (Oxford language dictionary). It's an act of self-preservation—creating an inward universe away from the outer world, which mimics what our cells also do to survive; they move in and thrive, and then they move out. Dissociation removes you from present time but never wholly separates you from what is happening around you. The outside world remains connected, interrelated, integrated. The inside world thrives in isolation.

*"Do you have any other advice?" asked the boy.*
*"Don't measure how valuable you are*
*by the way you are treated," said the horse.*
—CHARLES MACKESY

My parents' home was beautifully maintained, highly artful, sophisticated, and stimulating. I was surrounded by creative intellects, and I paid attention to them even if my academic record did not reflect that. My father inadvertently saturated me with his piano genius nearly every single day of my first seventeen years. Vanishing behind the closed door of my bedroom, his thrilling fingers scaled up and down the keys like the heart of a mad man's; he recalibrated my pulse and my breaths with his music, and I became his past, present, and future, whether I cared to or not. Classical compositions rose through my floorboards.

I came, habitually. Was I surviving or was I thriving? My father's hands. He introduced tempo, meter, crescendo; contrast, elegance, balance. Had someone betrayed him, traumatized him when he was young? Had the piano saved him? Perhaps he had been coded by, had experienced a trauma before me. Perhaps it was deeply buried within him. Perhaps it was as Suzanne Simard described in her interview "Forests Are Wired For Wisdom" (2021)—my father's superpowers of resilience, high-functioning intellect, and creativity seeped organically into the life and death of me, a beautiful, highly evolved, complex adaptive system of science and humanity.

I didn't play hide-and-seek much at my parents' house. There weren't as many clever places to hide, and we didn't have as much freedom to roam there, although the jungle safari of standing plants in my mother's room-sized, walk-in terrarium was enticing. It was a forest of smoky musk air and exotic earth. To hide in my mother's living room forest was to go on safari, hunt for treasure, hide from predators. But Bubby's attic offered me the truest escape and was where I longed to be most. All of the doors in Bub's house heaved and moaned when I pulled them; knobs and hinges crackled and creaked. But if I hitched the attic door up and to the right, nice and tight, I silenced its wooden protests and easily snuck into the spider dust of darkened light.

There was, after my eyes adjusted, a brighter spot from the window in the corner. The sea-tested steamer trunks slowly appeared resting next to Poppy's wobbly wardrobe. His long-ago worn suits inside hung below the odd-shaped hat boxes on the shelves, everything networked in insect lace. Against the wardrobe stood misfitted dining chairs with fraying lattice seats balancing burned-out lampshades. Rolled-up maps in cardboard containers stayed stacked underneath them. (*Heigh-ho, the places you did go hiding in your grandmother's cove.*) I acted like a pirate, a pilot, a violinist, a chef, a conductor, a steam engine driver, a cat. Eventually, my sister would decide if finding me and winning that round was worth her climbing the third-floor stairs and testing her fear of the attic's darkness. More typically, she bellowed her surrender from below, "Come out, come out, wherever you are," and "Tuni, you win. Come out."

I was four in my parents' living room. My mother watered the plants or talked quietly on the phone. My father was in his office, sucking on a cigar, chewing it, working or reading at his desk. I inhaled the cigar smoke where I sat nearby in my leotard and tights, on the velvet barrel chair, on the other side of the dividing wall. I was even softer than the velvet I sat on, in a shade of pink everywhere, my torso, my arms and legs. The neckline of my leotard rolled into a delicate curl over my collarbone, like a turtle's slow retreat. It tickled. Its long cotton sleeves reached my wrists, ladylike. My head bowed, my hands and fingers interlaced, at rest, in my lap, I sat.

I never cried.

I thought about the dance class I had just come home from, how many mistakes I had made. I tried to understand why my fifth position was easier that night and why it was harder to keep both heels on the floor and in line, turned out, in fourth.

He shuffled the papers on his desk. The shuffling and sliding of papers lifted my chin. Time to go to bed. I packed up my body shapes and the twists I was analyzing, the bends and arches I was remembering from class. I went upstairs and undressed, set my folded dance clothes on my white plastic rocking chair and put my nightgown on. I called from my room, "Mom, will you tuck me in?" And she did. She pulled up tight my sheet into a firm berm across the fronts of my shoulders and high under my chin. She folded the top sheet and blanket deeply underneath me, snug under the mattress. She tucked me in first, before he did. I lay on my back, immovable. I liked the embroidered loopy straps of my nightgown on my shoulders.

I knew his heavier step, the click and heaviness of his shoes, the shuffle between the steps. I watched as she stepped away from the bed toward the door, and I didn't move when he came into my room or when he took her place at my bed. I didn't move as he stood with his back to the door and slid his hand underneath my clean cotton sheet. I didn't move as I waited for his hand to find my thigh. "Good night," he said, touching, inching toward that place where he made good night circles with cigar-holding fingers.

I flew into Bub's attic; I hid in Poppy's wardrobe and in his old man suits with the arm cuffs down and low over my hands. His felted fedora slid over my squeezed-shut eyes in the dark. I counted the shutters along my windows while inside the wet sea bunk. I quietly stayed afloat in Poppy's wardrobe. I slept.

I grew very accustomed to the energy between my legs, the buzzing that traveled into my belly. I tapped it easily when I was in the living room, when I danced. I slid the barrel chairs to the sides of the room against the walls to make space. The fiberglass coffee table cubes and tiger rug, I stacked in the corners. The living room emptied of its furniture, I had room to flail and swirl and abandon my body. I pulled energy from the underworld below me—under the floorboards, under the earth—and brought a sanctuary directly into my home, like Bub's attic. I free-formed a portal toward safe expression; movement was the tool I used to harness protection.

My father's good night ritual, I had determined, was not truth. His hand testing the tops and sides of my thighs featherlight, his tiny tickle, back and forth, was a make-believe story I could close my eyes away from. Good night. My mother standing small in the hall was one of her God tricks. It wasn't her standing there in her mom clothes; it was her shadow. I counted windows. Eight in all.

As he stood, lingering at my bedside, I lay twitchy-backed with my dead fish closed eyes. Sometimes, I checked on the stuffed animals, like a peek, and they stayed animal-toy quiet on their rocking chair home: a squirrel, a kangaroo, a gopher. I rocked, between my thighs, despite them. Once or twice, I heard my mother call his name from my doorway, a lower version of her normal voice, like piss. And his half smile turned from me, his eyes darkly socketed, and left. "Good night, Tuner," he smoked out. And I can't remember ever crying. I didn't. I remembered the energy staying high in between my legs until I slept. I remembered fisting my baby scarf, silky security under the sheet, fire orange and thinly soft. That was the scarf my mother incinerated a few years later.

## *not a dream*

I stand at the edge of the seashore and slowly, with every riptide circling up the bank and ripping back down again, my feet sink farther in, my weight falls farther backwards and farther into the wettest, quickest sand. Light and energy curl and spiral at my heels, which draws my tailbone down and stakes me there at the endless sea. Her seaweed lair encircles me in a safe and salty hold, and I am transported to the other side of human life, to the other side of the horizon, where the dead await, where gods and goddesses stand by. And I never cried.

*See all human behavior as one of two things:*
*either love, or a call for love. . . . We are not held back*
*by the love we didn't receive in the past, but by*
*the love we're not extending in the present.*
—MARIANNE WILLIAMSON

I was five years old when I met Lincoln. His family lived behind the home my parents built in the suburbs, a land pit spaceship house. It was built at the bottom of a steeply graded hill, the first floor at street level, the basement two floors below. The driveway was a quick and dirty sideways switchback into the garage. A walking bridge led from the garage to the home. Its entryway connected to a circular layout like a donut, and the staircase was the hole in the middle—living, dining, and kitchen on top, bedrooms stacked beneath, basement bedrooms stacked beneath that. There were three hills that stood behind and to the right of our new home, and just beyond them, a catty-corner's hike through the field, lived Lincoln.

Lincoln's mom's hair was the exact same color as his: Celtic copper penny and cut short around her face. She was thin, like him, freckled, with a tiny overbite, tiny delicate nose, and dimples that made divots around her hitched-to-one-side smile. They both smelled of pine and corned beef and ivory soap. Even the dog smelled Irish.

Out back, Lincoln and I ran the hills, monkeyed up trees. We sat under the willows on the back side of the pond between our houses, braided the branches of sage-lipped leaves, tags winding and flipping, our camouflage, our game. Sitting knees, tall side-by-side at our thighs in worn corduroys and sucking lemon drops until our pockets emptied, he slowed my gaze over and over toward the ducks and algae, toward the sun catching and blinding the moment, coaxing my eyes out. Were his green? Like pine? Brown eyes? Dark, like heaven and soil and death forever? At night, we snuck quietly around the neighborhood, cut into tidied yards, picket-fenced or gnome-lined beds, young kids' toys stacked near a stoop. We zip-lined, tire swung, ran away. His eyes pointed north toward the lights, seafoam, emerald, lime, and citrine.

"What do you want to be when you grow up?" I'd asked him. He tilted and smiled, held the back door for me, walked past his mom presenting brownies or crackers and cheese or Twinkies, and replied, "A fireman, maybe, or forest keeper, I think. Forests. Fish. What do *you* want to be when you grow up?" I sat and watched his mother shift her gaze toward me. She smiled and said, "Have another."

In the winter, we sled the three hills between our houses. The uppermost hill was small, steep, and typically a sheet of ice. We hopped on a red flyer disc. "Tuck your legs under mine; hold your hands under my thighs." He hurried. Blinding white sky, switchback winds, we rushed.

The second hill's slope spilled out more slowly; our screams thinned as we pulled our breaths in more deeply. My legs squeezed tighter, his pressed in around mine, and we dueted courage, wicking awe and fear.

The final hill was a long flight down, a descent that would have us end either in the field or at pond's edge, depending on which lane the sled caught. Often, we built moguls in that third hill. And other times moguls were already there, built and left behind by someone else. We hadn't seen it before we hit it. My shriek sliced into his as the jump catapulted us. We hovered on the disc and then smash-landed. With my jaw fully locked open, my eyeball, cheek, and collar-bone bulldozed the packed snow and ice. "You okay? You okay? You okay?" he screamed, his boots and legs suddenly planted between me and the pond ahead. He pulled hunks and chunks of ice from my mouth, lowered and folded into me, wiped my tears, and, like a brother, carried me home.

When I was sixteen, the night before senior year in high school, sharing brown bottles of 3.2 Pabst Blue Ribbon, he said it that second time. "Let's kiss." In his backyard on the picnic table as the sky began to darken and the few first stars revealed themselves: "Let's kiss." And I brought my eyes to his. He'd said it the exact same way back when we were six or seven, in his blacked-out bedroom closet with our backs against the wall and our backsides on the floor; we leaned in, we hooked each other's breath, we pressed our mouths together like pancakes in prayer. But that night before our last year in school together, my lips met his in laughter, and that pseudo kiss ensured our properly non-intimate, ever-lasting love affair. We held hands and made toasts, just like best friends do.

I was there when he got married in Colorado after he graduated from Fort Collins. He got a job in forestry management. We held each other at his mama's funeral, our scents embracing the same as always, the clean bar of soap on spruce or scotch pine, baby powder; his dad had finally moved away from their home, left our pond and our hills. The thirty-six years between our last kiss and the night he died were otherwise mainly empty of us, our lives racing into different parts of the country, other ports of love, and family and everything. His time was shorter than we thought.

He was fifty-three when he died. He played pond hockey, the obituary read. He organized Christmas parties. He canoed, fished, hunted for rocks along Lake Superior.

Friends described him as a shooting star, fast and brilliant. Friends said they would miss his laughter.

I spoke with him the year before he died, after his wife had called me asking if I would contact him. She was worried about him. He was depressed. "Of course," I said. Lincoln and I swapped our bone-old fondness for each other; I listened for familiar, for dirty copper bangs and uncounted freckles, and we storytold. That last phone call I said, "I love you, Lincoln," and "I love you too," he said right back. "Just tired." *Don't be tired alone,* I thought.

In reflection, I've thought about the what ifs—have you? Imagining I have become . . . a wanderer, climber, doctor, chef, an ocean diver, space hunter, red light worker, trans, a politician—anything but me. *What if.* Habitually I return to a fish, a fish, and a fish, slippery and rippley, qwerky-ing into pockets of channeled rivers, engorged in briny fortune and unfettered flow. The underwater underworld where my body is buffered, cool, fast, and unholdable.

What if.

When I was nine, I chose Liza.

1972.

I watched Liza Minnelli in the film *Cabaret*. Liza. A carnal, black-lidded sea lion with a jet blaze of lashes dripping over crimsoned lips, a corset cinch of shiny skin. She French-curled and inhaled burning tips off her fags; she exhaled dirty rapture. Immediately after I saw the film, I cut off all my hair. Dropped off at a salon by my mother, I explained to the stylist Liza's hairstyle in *Cabaret*: a six-pointed pixie cut with one of the points slicing down the middle of the forehead, one long point posted in front and behind each ear, and the final point centered at the back of the skull.

The next morning, I stood at the corner across the street from my house and waited for the school bus. My flared cords were midnight blue and wind-pressed flat against my shins. I shifted from one Converse All Star to the other, a sway, a turtleneck quiver. I stepped up onto the bus. I kept my head down and counted off the dirt-streaked tennis shoes, the loafers, the wet crud of the bus floor, cushion innards poking through the red plastic seats, dark jeans, Wranglers. There were nickel-sized puddles along the metal frame of the rubber runner, the length of the bus. I crept along. Silenced, it seemed, by my entrance, the cliques paused before mobilizing, before systematically pairing and turning in their seats as I passed, head down, back of the bus.

My mother was likely still asleep, snuggling in her cotton nightdress tied at her collarbone, priggish, and drowsy, unfussed by the morning sun glancing at her. My father might have been standing at the nurse's station by then, already at work in his long white coat unbuttoned, brilliant fingertips, lifesavers. My mother might have mixed a dollop of foundation and Dove lotion together in the palm of her hand, dipped her fingertips in, painted her face. She might have poured her coffee and set the cup on her bathroom sink, pencil-lined her eyelids, and applied mauve lipstick down the upper right, down the upper left of her mouth, pursed her lips. I loved watching her apply lipstick. And my father, by the end of that day, would have come home late; he would have had rounds at a hospital, and everything he said would have been listened to very carefully, deferred to. I would have sidestepped his droopy, sad eyes and tall cutout silhouette and looked away from his glaring stare when he arrived home. I would have landed on their bed to watch television. I would have waited.

The elm and maple leaves danced across the bus window, and the rain drizzled off their leaf tips and hopped into the wind. I sat in the very back seat, the emergency exit seat, pulled my knees in, tucked my chin, lifted Liza sea-lion eyes forward. I couldn't hear what they were saying, but I watched as their hands shot up between their mouths for whispering secrets. "Slut," someone hissed as I stepped off the bus, that one time, loud enough.

I locked the door of my bedroom later that night and cut off the point in the middle of my forehead.

Other times I thought *what if*:
a doctor.
a rabbi.
a chef.
a baker.
a president.
non-gendered.
a carpenter.
a fish.

I was aware I was shameful, abnormal, footing a secret, *weird*. The idea of my being thought weird or strange consumed me. "You're weird." I heard it every day. "You're weird," from every direction, and I believed it. I kept a daily count.

Weirdo.
Slut.
Liar.

I started stealing my mom's things when I was eleven or twelve. Trinkets she decorated ledges with, trinkets on bathroom shelves, a tiny painted wooden doll. "Antonia," she cornered me, "have you seen my little angel?" and she pointed to the windowsill behind the toaster oven in the kitchen. "It was there yesterday. Now it's gone." And she froze at the spot, until large and hard enough to God me. "Where is it?" elevating. "No," I climbed on, lied worse, "I didn't take it," into a scream. And her, "I asked if you'd seen it, not if you took it," seeing me. And unable to back down because I'd lost the trick of truth telling, I shrieked, "I don't know!" I was a slut, a weirdo who masturbated, who touched herself and lied, who lied and stole, a floater, no strings.

I had given it to a friend earlier that day in school, a tiny painted wooden girl with wings holding a play ball with both hands. I had rolled the top of the brown paper bag over her and stuffed it in my jacket pocket, given it to a girl I liked. But my mother never misplaced things, and I had to ask the girl for it back. "You lied," she said as I handed it to her. "Didn't you?" she persisted. But I wasn't afraid of her. I hated her. She placed it back onto the sill where it belonged. "You're grounded."

I longed for mentorship, at least I figured that out many years later. I longed for shelter under a wing. But what occupied my brain most of the time then was the pleasure I enjoyed, served up in secret, by my father and by me. It was an ongoing message of wrongdoing, a shameful secret, a perverse, accepted, ho-hum routine.

I never ever believed in the concept of being *parented*. With her, I was in combat. I was a rival, an adversary. She once showed me how to sew, though, which in hindsight was a skill I was proud to have. But then, I really didn't want to learn how. "Come here and watch me do it," she said, and I got up from where I lay in between them and walked around to her side of the bed. She had glasses on, more than likely a second pair of glasses on top of her head. And with a sewing needle dangling from her lips like a cig, she side-talked sewing technique to me, grabbed the needle from her mouth and with the other hand daggered an end of the thread through its eye, pulled and matched up its two ends, pinched them before tangling them together, then tightly wound them a few times around the ends of two of her fingertips, and drew down the little mess until it surfaced as a knot, like magic. One index finger was thimbled, a tiny silver messenger cap. She stretched the fabric, turned it inside out—a sock, or underwear, a shirt—and carefully stitched up holes, teeny tiny stitches, perfectly aligned, formed new seams, barely visible, without pucker or loose threads, darned. And when finished and the item was turned right side back out again, the hole had vanished; the tear or worn-down part was non-existent. I liked the tying the knot part best. And I liked getting my socks back without the holes in the heels or toes. But I wasn't looking forward to being old like her and lying in a bed with a stack of clothing to sew and two pairs of glasses on.

Grounded, in my bedroom, on my bed, I placed the palm of my hand on my chest. I rested my other hand over the first one. I knew who I was (a liar, a stealer, a weirdo, a slut) and felt fairly certain most everyone else knew too.

I never told anyone what my father did. Nor did he. We grew into early adolescence together, with our unspoken details.

I was six, seven, eight, nine, ten.

Eleven.

Dr. Gannon was played by Chad Everett in my favorite show, *Medical Center*. Before the nightly news, we watched the hospital drama together on their king-sized bed. I could see them reflected in the windows; I could see us colored in TV blue. My father had a book near, a medical journal. My mother sewed or if the phone rang, talked into the mouth-piece, spiral-corded yellow, wedged between her ear and shoulder. I hard crushed Dr. Gannon in skintight slacks, suede shirt, and sunglasses. I hard crushed the wide satin choker around his neck.

I lay between them, tucked my feet underneath their pillows, and waited for my father's hand on my ankle or higher, my father's hand at my bottom or under, a circle and slow, a tickle. I became impatient with him, asked for him, out loud, for tickles. And she watched. And she spat his name out, eventually, and reined us in. I was conspiratorial. We were.

Joe Gannon had thick pork chop sideburns, a side-combed, side-parted sexy man hairstyle; his chin was always tipped down so his wet saucy eyes could look up into mine. The nurses loved him. He looked like my dad.

She normalized it. Her acquiescence condoned it. My terribly fragile, broken, godless, duteous, rigidly intellectual, meek mother was guilty of knowing, and sewing. My father was blameless.

The three of us on their bed, she pulled another set of white socks to darn, another lump of underwear to mend. On some nights, when she decided to put down her needle, I moved away from him, asking, "Can I lie on your tummy, Mama?" and I lay fully on top of her, my stomach to hers, the side of my face near her breasts, and her heartbeats double rhumping and thumping. Her misery needed me; I felt sure she was unknowingly begging for me. And I proceeded to jump into her heart thumps, over and over, rode her beat, found her, found us there, neither of us willing to speak.

For the Christmas holiday, we decorated a tree. Her ornaments were exotic, miniature works of art: paper Chinese
lanterns and painted metal windmills. Shimmering silver
tinsel hung from aluminum mandalas or from vibrant-col-
ored Huichol God's eyes, yarns in hot pink, neon yellow,
bright orange, and green.

I met Santa. I wore navy knit tights and a tartan sleeveless
dress, a navy turtleneck, a pea coat with leather toggle buttons,
patent leather shoes. I handed my coat to my mother and
walked up to Santa's knee, and he patted it and offered me a
pink, puffy hand before picking me up then with both of his
and bouncing me on his plush, jolly thigh. "And you are . . ."

"Tuni," a whisper in the basement of the mall.

"Of course you are!" and I bobbled and nodded my head
on top of him. "Well, Tuni, I do hope you've been treating
others as you wish to be treated. Ho, ho, ho."

I stared at his old gray beard, the hairs from his nose, his
tiny specs. "What?" I whispered, terrified.

"In order to get presents! Ho, ho, ho!" he carried on. "Do
unto others, HO *HO*!" My mother's mantra, she'd said it a
thousand times. Do unto others—the golden rule, the only
poem I was made to remember, like a law. Unattainable. Non-
sensical. I watched as my sister bounced on his knee, and he
laughed the same as he did with me, and she laughed too and
nodded and bobbled and smiled and spoke quietly to him.

In the afternoons I took ballet lessons with Miss Raya Lee.
The ballet center where she taught was on Hennepin Avenue,
on the second floor of an old brick building in uptown
Minneapolis. I double jumped the steep stairs up, used them
to ready my limbs, my core. Black short-sleeved leotard, pink
tights, worn and rosined pink leather slippers, hair slicked

back tight and pinned—a coiled snake caught by a net. I sat in the lobby on the floor before class, the radiator in front of me, and wedged both of my feet underneath its heat, then used the hot cylinders to curl my baby bones, the obsession to obtain perfection—a deeply arched point. I halved myself. Folding forward from my pelvis, I laid my torso onto my legs and rotated them away from one another like slicing down the belly of a fish, flipped my inner thighs out. Shaky breaths slowed as my stretch deepened. I was fully inside my self, creating the possibility of broadening, expanding, magnifying, widening, blooming—my ultimate mantra, my ultimate love.

When Raya arrived, her long blond mane was loose, blanketing the length of her spine, landing at her tail where the small of her back swooped. "Come in, girls," she said softly, holding the door open as the previous class filed out. We arranged ourselves, composed attention. With my left hand wrapping the wood barre, I breathed and passed through, leaving behind the ordinary.

I memorized;
amended.

To my left, in the mirror, I watched my big toe as it slid forward on its callous, through rosin, tendu. Turning away from the reflection, I squeezed my bum, switched my focus toward my pelvic bowl, lit it, lengthened, remembered to ignite the shield over my belly. My thighs flayed as they had when I stretched before class, but now actively they strained to turn beyond what I could achieve, my soft bones aching to reshape themselves, to sacrifice themselves for the art form. Tendu. Then first. Then tendu. Then first. Obedient. Beautiful.

I didn't talk much back then; I barely *dialogued.* Instead, I discovered how to communicate with my body.

I began masturbating irreverently, constantly, out of control. At night, during the daytime, weekends, behind my locked bedroom door, or in my tiny bathroom, climaxing. When no one was nearby, I humped the edge of my parents' bed until rawness bloomed on my sex.

One day, I noticed my father had stopped. His blatant erotic touching had ended discreetly, just as it had begun. Raya, my teacher, left the ballet center and relocated to a studio out of town right around that same time. I began having stomach aches, doubling over in pain before going to classes. I quit. "You cannot *not* do something," my mother said. "If you're going to quit ballet, you'll do something else, study gymnastics. Or you'll go to theater school; you'll audition for the Children's Theatre School." In a folding chair in the corner of a cold field house, I sat with my mother and watched her watching the girls, the gymnasts. She was hunched over her purse, rubbing her fingers together, squeezing her elbows, chalking, flipping, flying.

"I'll try out for theater school," I said.

The Children's Theatre Company and School. Contemporary, modern, elegant, clean, a glass-doored lobby, an elevator around a corner, chrome, white brick, three levels of professional (and brilliant) actors, singers, dancers, artists. A number was pinned onto my back, my black leotard, my name checked off. Surrounded by hundreds of hopefuls, warming up vocals, legs, pacing, I stared ahead until I sang, memorized choreography and monologues. I got the acceptance letter in the mail.

In order to attend theater school, I was registered into a citywide urban arts program that enabled me to get academic credits for singing, acting, and dancing (my life away). My sixth-grade education was pared down to three classes a day: science, math, and English. By the time I was a senior in high school, I was down to two courses: English (a Shakespeare class that I ironically failed) and choir. Monday through Friday, I two-stepped out of my high school building's front door by noon, leaving behind pimpled, hormonal, and excessively blond girls in cardigans and blouses clique-huddling at their lockers. I left behind boys' jerseys worn by smitten girlfriends of boy jocks, down the hall from the lizarding greasy-haired potheads congregating in the bathrooms, dirty handsomes in their matted bangs and chew-dipping smiles, buzzed. I forfeited Led Zeppelin slow dances, pep rallies, high school musicals, and every team sport. I had no idea what Friday night football games were, which inadvertently solidified my weirdness, my sluttish reputation. Up the hill from school, I hiked daily to the bus. My nose pressed against the dirty bus window, I watched the landscape throughout the school year color and brown, die and be born again. I transferred downtown to a second bus and landed at the corner of Third Avenue and Twenty-Fourth Street, the Children's Theatre Company and School; a black leotard and a plié, the alto section in the second row, sitting on the floor of a darkened room practicing relaxation techniques with my eyes closed. A different world.

"What's your name?" Sylvia, the ballet mistress, asked. Her dog, Toto, asleep at her feet, furred chin heavy on his paws, smelling of cigarette smoke. Sylvia opened and unfolded her arms, her wings, and sized me over. "Stand there, behind Bonnie, in front of Nance." She threw down from the beginning, sandwiching me in between two of her favorites. Corrections came steadily from her rigid lips. Her hollowed hips initiated her pointing arms and hands, and prodded her fatless legs, her slender knees, and her knobbed feet forward. She finger-pushed corrections into my flesh, unimpressed, and I began to fear making the smallest of mistakes, tried desperately to remain on count, which was a big problem for me, for I had a habit of being behind, late for the next count. I sometimes daydreamed.

Her favorite student, Bonnie, was everything she was not. Bonnie had thick, heavy black hair and supple curves that softened her everywhere. She was ethereal, a young girl's gossamer dress. Her extensions reached the stars, her arches were nautilus shells, her arabesques kissed the bun on the back of her head. I tried very hard to be Bonnie.

But the theater school was truly a circus, a wild and genius world of imagination and creation, smoky mirrors, sleights of hand, comedies, tragedies, tea parties of misfits, marionettes, puppeteers. It was known citywide for its pedophilic theatrics that occurred behind the scenes of its queerly brilliant and exotic high art; understood but hidden, hushed and ignored by many (including my parents, including so many parents). Within the first couple of months of joining the school, I was asked to replace someone in the main stage production of *The Ugly Duckling*; it was my "first break." After an audition, I was chosen again for the next show that season, *Pinocchio*, and so on. A two-month run of one production followed another two-month run—rehearsals, tech weeks, and suddenly I was on a never-ending loop, finishing with nine shows a week, from Tuesday to Sunday. My schoolwork might have been done on the floor of the theater house when I wasn't needed on stage during a rehearsal. My schoolwork might have been done in the dressing room or the green room on break in between performances. My schoolwork was rarely done.

But deviant sexuality was *done*, everywhere, in the dark in the wings, behind the scrim, in dressing rooms, or above the theater in an office, behind a curtained window. The children of the theater learned from and worked with the professionals, their teachers, their mentors who also happened to be their castmates, their fellow performers, their ensemble, and sometimes their predators. I did not feel *weird* anymore. And I wasn't aware of ever being called a slut.

"*Mom,*" I said sharply after flicking my bedroom light on, exposing her in my closet behind its nearly shut door, chin tucked, spine bent, holding my open diary, snapping it shut, turning toward me.

My mother didn't love her mother. She told me this, many times. She said, "She was a terrible mother. Her notions, her life, everything was more important than I was," and "I did everything for her, and she never thanked me, never acknowledged how I supported her."

"Mom," I escalated, "what are you doing?" and stepped toward the antique glass doorknob on my closet door to open it wider, the knob that matched all the others in her home, the knobs she scoured antique shops for all over the Twin Cities in order to replace the knobs that were previously there. I pushed the door in toward her where she stood reacting to the light I had just turned on.

My mother did not have the experience of tenderness with her mother; she did not share intimacy with her, collapse into her, celebrate her, trust her. I wish I would have known that early on, understood the messiness of her childhood. I wish she would have told me how sad she was. I wish I would have known that before I was born.

She held the diary out to me, angrily. "I already know all of this," she hissed, which I knew was a lie because she knew nothing about me. "It's trash," she growled. So I ate her. I ate her guilty hand, her hair, her spine, her heart. I ate myself too, the unicorns, the broken hearts, the ladders out, and the dreams. "Tell me what you've written about! Tell me!" I heard her wail as I spiraled toward the underworld, a tiny speck.

Even with her scoliotic spine and the challenges it presented in my mother's sophisticated fashion choices, she curated an extensive collection of clothes. Billowing silks and forgiving linens, elastic-waisted skirts, and pants paired with modern tunics categorically sorted and hung on heavy steel hangers, front to back aligned, casual, business, elegant. And in the adjacent corner cedar closet was her store of wools and furs. "Can I dress up in the red fur?" I had called out to her in her study, dutifully adding, "Please?"

"May I," she corrected, "and it's not red fur, Antonia. It is a red *fox.*" Unfurling her slump from where she sat at her desk, she reassembled herself into governess, the lawmaker, my ruler. Once in the bedroom she pushed me aside and retrieved the garment bag the fur was hanging in, laid it flat on her bed before unzipping it, carefully. "Go ahead," she said, "I'll wait." She wore her fur coats when attending symphonies or opening nights at the theater, jeweled, hair teased and sprayed, a beaded clutch or a satin one in her suede or leather gloved hand.

"That's okay," I demi-smiled as I turned my chin up toward hers, "I don't want to anymore," and exhaled; I was learning cat and mouse. "I'll hang it back up." Her eyes squinted sweetly at mine; her smile tightened.

She handed us her credit card, and my sister and I climbed out of her car for our once-a-year shop for school clothing—this year for my sixth-grade wardrobe. I picked out a pair of brown polyester pleated and cuffed pants with narrow cream pinstripes. The pantsuit had a matching buttoned vest with a silky back and a jacket. I modeled it for my mother as soon as we returned home from the mall, pivoted in front of her, pulled the collar of the jacket up toward my face, and fashioned cat eyes on her. She crossed her arms over her chest and placed her weight squarely onto her back hip, prepared to strike. "It doesn't look good on you." First hit. "It's a man's suit. Why would you wear a man's suit?" Follow up. "It's not becoming at all on you, in fact." Bullseye. "You look like a dyke." Straight through the heart.

I had no idea what "dyke" meant, but it didn't matter; she sounded evil, which meant I was bad. It made her skin turn gray when she said it, her nostrils flaring, her finger twitching. I remembered taking the suit off downstairs, quietly retreating, and locking myself in my bedroom, small and cold and filled with her disgust in me. I remembered I had laid it on my bed, flat and perfect, and decided I would never wear it, at least not all together as I had shown her. I wore the slacks. I wore the jacket. And I wore the vest. But never together.

My childhood home was beautiful, with beautiful things placed on beautiful furniture, beautifully. A white marble dining room table with matching side tables, modern chrome legs standing underneath them, sculpturally grand. Smooth velvet barrel chairs also chrome legged, with circular wide chrome discs as feet—modern and elegant. On fiberglass cubed coffee tables were perfectly placed vintage glass paper weights, globes that were heavy in my hand and cool on my face. Hundreds of seashells were set and ordered by shape, color, size precisely—sailing chambers of nautilus, creamy-eyed cowries, sea cones with intricate crosshatch mosaics. My favorite, and she had only one, was the "Venus comb" in the palm of my hand. She was covered in hundreds of spines, prickly and delicate; I'd looked it up: the goddess of love used them to comb her long hair (*do not touch* was handwritten on a simple folded white note card nearby). One of those marble side tables was saved for all of those corals and shells, her dry sea.

Statues of every sized Buddha hid amongst her towering and rare indoor plants or on cherrywood shelves encased in glass. Buddhas grew out of ivory and horn or jade or bronze or carved walnut, armies of them. I dusted their fat bellies carefully. I picked shells up from the table in sections, air brushed the dusting cloth over them, replaced them exactly back again; these things were her church, wiped clean on Sundays.

For long hours my mother sat at her desk working, and unless I had permission, I was not allowed to touch it or anything on it. But "Yes, you may," she sometimes uttered when she was distracted, and I reached into the bottom drawer where I knew she kept the baby books. I sat by her feet on the floor, ankles crossed with my baby journal in front of me. Inside of it was a small envelope holding the first snip of my baby hair. As she pressed and pushed papers above me, I rechecked my baby weight and height, the time of my birth. Taped onto one page, my favorite page, was a small Kodak photograph of me, my dark pressed-in face framed in a few wisps of hair, wearing a barely visible lace dress, a collar at my neck.

I couldn't picture my mother little. I couldn't picture her happy. I couldn't picture her at the heels of her mother, sitting on the floor beside her, with her.

She remained quiet at her desk, writing, bent over. My eyes rested on her hunched back. One side hitched higher than the other, a hard shell, mother turtle. Once in a while, an almost muted moaning escaped her when her spine's collapse overwhelmed her. She tried most things to correct it: the fiberglass corset, steel rods surgically inserted to prop up and support each side of her spine, fusions. Nothing erased her hump. Nothing relieved her pain. Maybe the doctors did save her from folding completely in half. Maybe, without them, she would have fallen completely apart.

---

*I imagine her attempting a stretch, a mindful posture, taking her body into her own hands, a lean into light, a press of inner faith. Her lack of self-care bolstered her harsh judgment of the world, emboldened her harsh judgment of others. "We can connect," I wish I could say to her, our physical selves, our cellular energies toward a mutual global self, our universal energy. "We can link, Mama, the flaws of our human physicality with the expanse of spiritual wholeness. Our egos battle, Mama, and detach us from connecting not only to ourselves but to each other. Our egos, Mama, resist love. Our egos don't love us, Mama."*

She said, "I never loved my mother," while looking down at me where I sat, cross-legged, memorizing the details of my birth.

Mama was a matte brown eyeliner a quarter-inch wide along the edge of her eyelid. She was foundation, a soft cream color smoothed over by both hands on hairless skin, her three middle fingers sliding gently down the sides of her nose and then back up again, landing where her high cheekbones slotted into her hairline. "I don't have makeup on," she'd say when I told her I thought her makeup looked nice. "I don't have any on."

She was beautiful. Men wanted her, lined up for her—she told me so. And when my father had stolen those gawky glances at her breasts in the elevator of the hospital where he was in residence and she had a desk job, she responded to his invitation for a coffee at the diner down the street with a nod yes. And at the Waldorf-Astoria a year later, she wore a tight bodice dress made of crepe with a proper high neckline, paneled shoulders, sheer puffed sleeves, and rhinestones cuffing her wrists. Pale pink satin shoes matched. Only her lip shade differed in color, a dark, ruby red.

It was a small nuptial; only close relatives attended. And very soon after, her firstborn, my brother, arrived. "What was it like when you started having babies, Ma? Do you remember it?"

"Nope," distracted by her needle and thread, she mumbled, "woke up and there you were. A perfect American beauty rose." Everything perfect. But she had no memory of a small human filling and then wriggling its way through her canal, the dam unlocking, her insides breaking apart. Maybe that would have changed her perception of self, if she could have witnessed her miracle making.

She was a 1950s opium-drugged baby maker. She wouldn't know how to describe her son's crowning or the piercing and slicing between her legs, the unimaginable pressure of a baby plowing through bone. She wouldn't have memory of her breaths culminating and harmonizing with the sacred whelps of her creations. "I remember going to sleep," she said.

I wished, when I had delivered my firstborn and all the ones that followed, that she could have piggybacked me during those sacred pushes, those fucking miracles. Perhaps that might have shifted her in some way, opened her heart more toward ravishment, ecstasy, wonder, exposed her to the sacred rawness of flaws and magic. I wondered how she would have reacted to a suckling infant on her breast. Had she ever caught awe with one of us in her arms? Had she inhaled us, our tiny paws, our squints and squawks? Had any of us cracked light into her bitter? For a moment?

She flushed her shit away quickly, before standing up off the toilet; there was never proof, in my lifetime, of her moving her own bowels.

She traveled behind her Mr./Dr., co-creator physician-man wherever his stethoscope and paycheck carried him. Every two years, another baby, every two years, another move; she transitioned into bigger homes, better schools, different parts of the country.

She was only thirty when I, her final baby, was born. She was still beautiful but also beautifully silent, buckling under her twisting, weakening spine.

Five decades later, aside her remaining Buddhas and books, near her African beads, next to her poodle, she agitated, adjusted the figurine on the table next to her, a minisculimeter to its left. She lasered her Lasiked eyes onto invisible specks of nothingness. She was a fall risk; she had fallen more than once in pursuit of invisible specks of air. She bruised her ribs when she fell reaching for dust. She scraped a cheek when reaching for schmutz and falling. "I am completely stable," she insisted, because if she didn't remember her falls, which she didn't, they didn't happen. Still, "What is that in the corner above the lamp?" she'd snap.

Standing up quickly, I moved toward where her finger pointed. "I got it, I got it," I said, balancing my loyalty, my wish to soothe and understand her, support her, and keep her safe with my sadness about how much she was faltering and narrowing and weakening. She was isolated, in part because she was the last one standing alive—she had outlived her husband, her best friends, her relatives—but also in part she was isolated because she stiff-armed and rejected people. She boxed up people according to her perceptions of their strengths and shortcomings, but in her eyes their weaknesses stood out more, their *failures.* Loneliness never consumed her; bitterness did.

"I'm sorry," she never said to me.

And out loud in return I never said, "I forgive you." But I did. I forgave her. Fuck. I never told her. Fuck. She never said it.

I was not separate from love. My mother and my father were not separate from love; none of us were. Shit happened; everything was shit. Everything happened, melodiously, cacophonical—like a dream.

"While you're there, darling, can you bring me a Sprite?" she sang. *It's not fucking Sprite*, I thought, once again. It was diet Sprite. I detested diet Sprite.

In becoming myself, I compulsively, like her, finessed my homes, moved little saved bits inches over one way or another until I exacted its essence. As pillows rested intentionally angled in her apartment, mine did as well in my house; placement was dictated by color, dimension, texture. By vibe. I was well suited to help her, tidy her, organize her, and she knew it.

She stared ahead at the portraits that hung on the wall. "It's exceptional, isn't it," she announced. "I am blessed to have this beautiful wall, these delicious photos right here in front of me."

And I stroked her, coddled her, "Very blessed, Mama."
Her dead friends and family members, her prejudices of
them, were set in stone. Her thirteen grandchildren were
arranged into a different montage nearby, elegantly framed.
And though they were young adults now, they were pictured
there on her wall when they were toddlers or adolescents,
photographs she'd selected to showcase them pure, when
they were impressionable and doting.

It had been three years since my father's touch, his smooth
skin circling cigar ash at the tops of my thighs. Only I had
replicated those sensations since he stopped. I was the one
recreating the padiddling of my clit.

When I was fourteen, I landed my first lead role at the Children's Theatre in the production of *Aladdin*. I was Jasmine, Aladdin's princess.

One late night after a Friday night performance, Gorgo, the lead performer, suggested I crash on his sofa at home. We had a matinee the next day, Saturday, and that way I'd get more sleep. My parents okayed it. "Yes, his girlfriend will be there," I had said. I slept on the floor under a quilt in the apartment's living room. Gorgo and his girlfriend slept in the bedroom.

The next morning, I'd heard them, their intimacy, their voices saying, "I love you." I heard her shuffling, her leaving through the front door.

"Tuni, come in here and lie with me," he had said, and my eyes snapped open. "Tuni, come here and warm up before we need to go." I loved him, Aladdin. In his early twenties, a professional actor with the company and an instructor in the school, he had an airy voice, large dark eyes, and long golden eyelashes lighter than his wavy copper hair, smoother than his pale freckled skin. He was slim and muscular. I left the quilt on the floor and stood. I was wearing my black leotard and a navy cutoff T-shirt, socks pulled high above my knees;

I entered his room. "Come in," he whispered, "come here." Without moving from his lie, he held the blanket over the open side of the bed, low—maybe his bed was on a platform, or maybe it was a mattress on the floor; it was low. I turned away from him, lowered myself to my knees, then hip, and with my hands for balance, slid underneath the blanket he held, onto my right side, a fetal baby girl, I curled in. I felt the blanket fall over my left shoulder, my back to him, and the yellow sheet bunching underneath me. I crossed my arms over my chest, placed my hands together. Breaths. I breathed. He spooned me, reached over my back and pulled my hand back with his. Heat was mounting behind me; I felt heat. He pulled my hand back and wrapped it onto and around; he squeezed my hand around his hard self, his manhood. I didn't know. I wasn't looking. My back was to him. He was behind me. My stomach clenched. He didn't speak. I closed my screaming eyes and claimed my hand, pulled it back like a shadow. But I was dust.

He pulled my leotard over to one side behind me. I felt his fingers in the crack of my tiny, tiny ass; I felt his fingers slip under my leotard. I was stone. He adjusted it, again; it had slipped, I had felt it slip, but he slid it back again. He wedged the fabric into my baby tiny crack and tucked it under. I was stone. He squeezed in, he pushed it in, inside me, behind me, he stuck, he pulled out, he pulled partway out and then dug into me again. He didn't speak. The room was silent red. I was red, my eyes, behind them, matching the room. There was gas in my . . . I felt gas in my mouth. He wasn't talking. Words vanished. I was a ghost without limbs, without a tongue; he sliced inside, the flesh of me. *Please stop. Please stop.* My words vanished. My brain washed black. "No" was under my tongue. "No" was at the bottom of my throat. He wasn't talking. He cracked me open, and my eyes shattered and my tongue dissolved, and I was stone and dust.

*no*
*don't*
*no*
help
*no*
*don't*
please
*no*
*don't*
no


just silence.
and he left.

I waited a few moments and then I pulled my leotard back
into place, proper, and held still.

I walked back to the theater beside him. He was talking,
talking, talking. My thighs were rubbery, burning and rubbing, raw and hot, sticky and slippery. In the dressing room,
in the basement, I put my stage makeup on. We were not
in the same dressing room. I was with the harem girls, my
harem. My face, neck, arms, and hands were painted Kabuki
white. My forehead and eyelids were painted red and pink.
The harem girls didn't paint their bodies white like I did,
because I was Jasmine, Aladdin's princess. I went to the bathroom once before pulling my white spandex bodysuit on and
noticed the blood on my thighs.

*don't*

On the toilet, I held the piece of toilet paper with blood on it. "Jill?" I wasn't crying. She was a harem girl. "I think I got a period?"

Aladdin.

Saturday.

Makeup.

"Yeah, okay, hold on," she said, and brought over a tampon, held it under the toilet door.

*don't.*

Blood.

Jill zipped me into the white princess.

I performed twice that day. Stayed in the dressing room in between shows. Washed my makeup off, pulled on sweats. I went home that night near midnight and slept. Woke up the next morning and performed two more shows that Sunday, a matinee and an early evening show. Curtain call up, curtain call down, hands up, hands down. I stepped forward, Gorgo stepped forward; our fingers laced, we bowed together, a curtain call.

"Do you feel okay? Are you coming down with something?" my mother asked when she pulled into the garage that night after bringing me home from the theater.

"No," I lied, "I'm fine."

There were several more weeks of Aladdin's run. I stopped eating. Stopped going to school. Stopped talking. Wrote in my diary, went to dance classes, performed in other productions, memorized lines, smoked. The school year finally ended. I quit. I left the Children's Theatre Company and School. I left high art and tea parties, pedophiles and child molesters.

It wasn't my period after all. I didn't bleed between my legs again until after my nineteenth birthday, five years later.

My parents owned a small piece of property on Martha's Vineyard and on it, two small cottages. From the time I was five years old, we traveled there and stayed from June through August, handing over much of our time to Jungle Beach, Lucy Vincent Beach, our beach—all the same. In the mornings that summer, painfully thin, I dressed myself for the beach, alone, away from my two sisters, in our bathroom. Underneath the extra-large boxer shorts (stolen from my father's laundry pile), and the extra-large Hanes V-neck T-shirt (same), I wore my kelly-green camisole leotard, cinched low at the sternum, seamed and snug; it held me together, like a friend. I swam in the sea. My father's shirt and shorts clung heavily in the waves, drenching me, my drunk-in-water legs sinking into the soft sand below, the clothing like stones frantically pulling me down. The wind decorated the horizon with indigo and curly-topped foamy white caps. And the wind spittled and spat all sizes of rocks and mussels and weeds and sea glass onto and into the beach and precious and falling clay cliffs. And the wind sang with the cawing gulls, wave over wave, and lifted the scurrying feet of sandpipers and plovers and terns and mergansers, feathers wet and matted but quick and flight ready. And the wind and the wind and the wind consoled me, consorted with me. Answered me. I hated everything but the wind.

After my departure from the theater and before I arrived on the Cape that summer, I attended a ballet camp. It was there I took my first jazz dance class. It was there I moved my body alongside the melody of Stevie Wonder's "I Wish"— barefoot, low to the ground, feet wide, hips grinding. It was there I was taught to pay attention to lyrics, the bass line, the back tracks—the soul. It was there I connected my soul to the soul of rhythm and blues.

It was also there my camp roommate taught me how to intentionally throw up. Bulimia. I had accidentally walked in on her after dinner in our bathroom. Hunched over the toilet, there she was, head submerged into the toilet bowl, her finger jammed and damming the back of her throat, a spastic groan wedging open her mouth. "Finished," she clucked, and then asked in her "t"-chopping, mouth-forward Brooklyn accent, "Do you want to me to teach you?" She pinched a small chunk of puke from her bangs and flicked it.

"Sure, I guess so," I said. I was barely eating anyway.

I was a natural, so simple. Just a tickle to my uvula and an index finger below my swallow. By the following week I wasn't keeping a single meal in my gut for more than half an hour. In the following years my bingeing morphed into advanced food restricting and denials, scale weighing before and after daily, bi- and tri-daily vomits; each time I felt sure it was more than food I was banishing from my body: I was murdering; I was a murderer. I was mutilating trespassing hands and carving open a hot prick. *Get out.*

I wasn't self-destructing, I was taking control, I was insourcing my true light. I knew I had become a predator. I wanted to be the predator more than anything. I wanted control.

*Better a sparrow, living or dead, than no birdsong at all.*
—CATULLUS

I suffered from bulimia until the day I learned I was pregnant with my firstborn son. For thirteen years I allowed and then vanquished food, every day. But when I was presented with the journey, the transition into caring for, the responsibility of another life, I chose him. I never ever stuck my finger down my throat again.

I had finally experienced ecstatic, out-of-body, reciprocal love—reciprocal lovemaking, a man's fiery love, a man's guttural love. His responses to me anticipated me. Enya's *Watermark* from beginning to end in the background, I had waited for him that first time in my apartment, in the living room, smoking, anticipating him, standing to look out the window, helpless to do anything but wait. Enya's *Watermark* on a loop, a CD, just one more song and then he'd arrive; a musical countdown to him, from the beginning one more time. I pressed play, and he still hadn't arrived. Enya's *Watermark*, stunning and pure, haunting echoes rose and fell, lush, synthesized chords blended into her trancelike vocals inside me, smoky in my lungs; again, I played her from the beginning, exhaled. I needed, I prayed for him to arrive, that first time, that first time, I wanted him to become her, ride Enya and slip into her, join me in her flow, my longing.

He came, late, hours late, hours later, pained in his apology, suited in sorrow and begging forgiveness; his tempo, his timetable, like hers, like Enya's, but rhythmically also his own, languid to start, "Forgive me," he said, "for being myself, for making you question." And his raw heart like her hand drum, a crescendo, his hungry soulful manner the ocean at night, darkly glossed in calm until turbulent, tumbling in our bodies. Our firstborn son, my firstborn son, taught me. My firstborn son taught me no.

I was radically thin. Bodysurfing far from shore, I waited for the perfect wave to approach me. The spacing in between each wave was crucial in determining whether it was the right one; was its lift high enough to sail on but not frightening or treacherous? I turned my body sideways preparing to swim in front of the next crest, to catch and beat its crash. If I timed it right, I would join its peak, and slipping it under my ribs and hips, fly, rush, and slam over-under, onto myself and into the sea until buried into the sand and shell, the rock, until sucked back with the riptide. I got rumbled and raked in the weeds, sucked into an ocean vortex.

Spent, I pulled myself from the watery hold, wrung out the oversized shirt, drained buckets and barnacles from the shorts. I averted my eyes from my parents, their books in their laps, as they stared at my bloated face, my hidden body, the illusion of my teenage figure underneath a father's underwear.

That summer, in the parking lot of Jungle Beach, I picked up what I thought was a local island paper. It wasn't. Weirdly, it was a neighborhood newspaper from Minnesota, my home state, folded, flattened, and sand crushed. A photograph of dancers popped out from the print, arms in L shapes, legs to the sky. I had never heard of them: The Minnesota Jazz Dance Company. I ran over to my mother who was packing beachy things, chairs and buckets, into the car, and pressed the paper into her hands. "They're having auditions." I pointed to the photograph and said, "I'm doing this."

I was hired. Zoe was the MJDC dance director. A red-headed, Southern-born, quick-snapping coach, she talked out of the side of her mouth, an unzipped corner that spoke jazz, bebop, blues, and funk; a whole new language, a whole new soul. It wasn't natural to me in the beginning; I was modeled in ballet, but slowly it opened me up, one well-fought step at a time—the shapes and patterns, the innuendos, the improvisations of jazz, sensual athleticism, syncopated footwork.

She was kind. She believed in my potential from the start, and even though I was young, she demanded the same from me as veteran company members. I watched them carefully, cloned them. I mimicked their glances, hip sits, shoulder tips, pelvic thrusts, rib rolls, spine waves. I plagiarized them. And even though Zoe blueprinted strength, opened her self-assured wings for me to gain confidence under, my vulnerabilities at times devastated me. I could be in a zone one moment and inconsolable the next. But Zoe continually faithed me back. "Take a breath, Tuni," she whispered. And while the others watched, she focused on my success, " . . . step left twice before the right."

"Okay," I responded, slowing myself down.

At the end of the day, I would think through insights I might have had, the shifts I made in my body that improved my technique: a pirouette became a triple from a double when I changed the angle of my chin. Broadening through my sacrum improved the balance of my hips in an arabesque. Visualizations filled me as I began every movement and sustained every moment in my mind, which was as natural to me as riding an ocean. And now I was getting paid to dream.

My climb out of my self-imposed darkness, my cage of hate, was completely reliant on dance. When jazz dancers performed, they storytold, cracked their souls and stirred their emotions into their choreography. I didn't feel that same connection—or release—when I performed ballet. Ballet's rigid discipline, its perfection, anchored me. But in the style of jazz dance, I was able to let go and embody uninhibited expression of myself.

"Get out of the back corner and stand here," Zoe said one day, pointing to a spot in the front row of the studio, a spot right next to her. Afro jazz, lyrical jazz, funk, pop, hip-hop, Southern gospel, soul.

# part two-a

## COURAGE

*Life shrinks or expands in proportion to one's courage.*
—Anaïs Nin

I was seventeen when I walked into Gus Giordano's jazz dance company studio in Chicago, twenty-fours after the phone rang in Minnesota. They were offering me a job with their company. I'd performed with Zoe's company for almost two years at that point, while somehow managing to receive a cap and gown before leaving high school. With that one day's notice, I packed up my clothing and dance gear and arrived in Michael and Charlene's apartment, all arranged by the Giordanos.

Michael Mary was a funny, dirty blond, with tiny tight dirty curls, always gelled. He sing-songed with a lisp and melodied nonstop commentary about fuck all, from morning to the end of time. His dancing skills were good enough, but his relationships amongst the members of the company were masterful, provocative, boundaryless, and gorgeously raunchy. The male dancers in the company—because of Michael and Charlene, my other roommate—hung out often in our apartment, smoking pot, laughing, lounging. They were touchy, as in they couldn't be near one another without touching each other, like a pet, like lovers. They were playful, delicate, and masculine. Charlene was the mama bear, their angel.

As a nurse, Charlene's hours ran late into the night, which made it convenient for her to arrive home in time for a party. Nurse-white mid-thigh polyester-jam zip-up-the-front short cap- sleeved maid/nurse/supertight sexy flight attendant dress, she was always sassed, Betty Booped; she was ready for her boys. She had jet-black hair cropped on her square jawline and skin as white as her nurse's coverall.

Jeffrey was one of Michael's best friends along with Jeffrey's lover, Kenny, both exquisitely formed. Everyone with everyone, they circled each other with their Marlboro smokes and marijuana joints, their spangled shorts and powdery snorts, hot love and no-doze jokes. Charlene kept up, swept up, dialed up, filled up. I listened in the dark behind the walls of my bedroom. Tick, click, feet-toe clacking, tumbling in from the night, rolling guffaws carried in under my door, onto my bed. I listened as they finished their evenings huddled in the hallway or further away in the kitchen, a late-night feast. I imagined their bodies woven, braided together, a knotted embrace; their whispered dialogues became the wilderness across my ceiling, my walls, my visual lullaby before sleep.

Jeff and Kenny both epitomized flawless physical beauty. Every turn and bend of their flesh was shaped by the hours they spent perfecting the craft of dance. Round, full. Sculpted. Sacred geometry. Compellingly functional. When not dancing, their gestures, pauses, turns, and folds continued to emerge as effortless artistry. They sat together on the kitchen floor squeezed into their black jeans and T-shirts, which couldn't contain their grace. They tongued each other deeply, smoked gayfully, stunningly sexual. I hungered to see them make love. I longed to watch them kiss, to keep watching them, their bodies seamless, delicate, powerful. *Let me in.*

Jeffrey choreographed a piece to "Born to Be Wild," by Steppenwolf. The men wore full leather chaps, leather vests, and gloves. Primarily a men's piece, it was accented with only one woman. When I arrived at Gus's company, the female role had already been cast, but eventually I won my shot at the part and alternated in. To start, the men held me, took my thighs in their hands, and pressed me up and over their heads. As I shifted my weight backward, two dancers let go of my thighs and grabbed my ass, a low rider, a badass cruiser on her bike. The other two simultaneously moved from my thighs to my feet, high above their heads, a hot Harley bitch. They drove; I rode my boys and the stage.

Then all at once, their eight hands launched me into the air—and I flew. Landing on the stage, I spun and twirled back into the choreography and onto the floor in thigh-high boots, a black leather vest, a black unitard, and a black, wild and fringy wig. I rejoined the men, we coupled and bound, we pumped our hips together, we arched and curled into a single moving being, we slid and crashed into orgied layouts, curving undulating waterfalls until they lifted me up from the floor and I Harley-bitched once more.

Once while performing that piece, I had an out-of-body experience. I had been picked up backstage and had hit my music cue, but then suddenly I was no longer being held by the men; I was hovering above them, on the catwalk. Peering over the stage lighting equipment, I saw myself, and them, move onto the stage: "Born to be Wild." Time froze as I hung. Time froze as I watched us dancing below. I was thinned air, a Source, pure light. I was also afraid; I felt gripped by space. And then, just as suddenly, time jumped forward and I was back on my feet. I had returned to normal reality, and my steps were miraculously correct, undulating again, body electric. After the piece was over, I shook as the curtain drew closed. And when the curtain lifted again, our second call, I cried.

AIDS and HIV wove itself into that world, the virus of the eighties, scoffed at by many, ignored, disbelieved. Those afflicted with it were ostracized, demoralized, stereotyped, shunned, shamed, ridiculed, bullied. Many suffered alone. Many suffered long, dreadful, heinous illnesses. And just as Jeffrey and Kenny did, many of them died.

When I was eighteen, I attended a weekend-long conference for sexual abuse survivors. I rode a Greyhound bus to Wisconsin from Chicago and joined hundreds of victims of rape, date rape, molestation, sex crimes. I imagined us a burdened tribe: the beaten, shamed, and violated—the afflicted in pursuit of karmic cleansing and buzzing and bumping into each other at a Sheraton Hotel on Lake Monona.

Pairs of weary, glassed-over eyes sliced into mine when I looked up from the lobby floor. Cloaked women burrowed into their diminished egos, trudged behind their blackened spirits. Women unaccustomed to being respected and in need of direction or leadership or love sat in circles, held hands, and wept. And that sourness rose; it rose high within my throat and toward me from their open mouths, that dank bitter odor of the fouled. And with open wallets, they let fly whatever dollars were necessary to be fixed. Screaming was encouraged, while other conference attendees cheered them on. The wails of being taken in dark alleys, on country roads, and around street corners; in dive bars, on the el, and deep within the suburbs. The lovers who weren't lovers in lovers' bedrooms, the truckers truck-stopping, scouting oases. "Lift up your shirt!" one dirty soul screamed from a truck window. "Show me your titties, pretty mama." *Please*. Objectify me. I asked for it, didn't I? Because I looked like I wanted it, and I didn't say no, right? Because of my outfit, I asked for it, right? Because I didn't laugh or snarl or piss on the evil of you, the fucking horror of you. Nope. I didn't move a muscle.

I bought the book, a compilation of more storytelling—tales as old as the Bible. And I was realizing amongst those women that I was nothing special, I was one of an infinite number of female wildlife that stepped too close to a whistle, a wink, a drink, a come-on. My story was a bore, no big deal. Maybe even made up.

My overnight bag stayed packed. The next morning, I came down early to the lobby for a cup of coffee and watched the rain pill and slide down the tall glass walls of the café. Women I recognized from the day before slowly filled in the tables around me. I recognized my drained expression in all of their faces. But I couldn't hold still any longer to hear more of what happened to them, to learn more deeply how they felt. I wanted no part of their stripped-down-to-less-than-human experience. I couldn't bear any more. The truth was, I felt they were all to blame for what had happened to them, like I was, and that they should change their behaviors if they wanted to stay safe. Become the predator, not the kill. (Because the sluts of middle school prophecy was what was up; that was survival.) Fuck them.

Hell-bent on flipping the narrative, I became the dominant one. From nightlife's subterranean clubs and their concealed rooms in the back to daytime's health clubs and the tanning rooms up front; pizza parlors, grocery lines—every minute of every moment of every day—I was on the hunt. And if I wanted a sexual hit, I got one. Who was next? The end game wasn't assuring anyone else's pleasure; it was assuring me controlling mine.

"You won't always look like this," the therapist told me. Deep down I was so tired, trusted no one. The convention in Wisconsin only made things worse. So I found a therapist who lived just down the block from me, a walk-up in a rundown North Side Chicago neighborhood. "Trust me," she said, petting one of the dozens of feral-looking cats that came in and out of the home office she had created at the front of her apartment where she saw her clients and where I sat opposite her, "you'll have to learn how to be in the world after your beauty fades away. You won't get your way all the time, like you do now." One of the cats snuck in between my legs, pressed its ginger fluff against my shin. I kept losing count of how many felines there were, stalking ledges and edges, in the hallway behind her, on the top of her chair, in her lap where she stroked them, between my legs. "You won't be getting second looks, gawks, and stares. It will," she snapped her fingers, and the cat jumped, "one day disappear."

*Fuck off!* I screamed in my head. "I don't really think that will happen," I said coolly.

"Well, sweetie," she continued, "there will be others coming up the pipe, and as your face softens and doubles under your jaw like mine did . . . I used to be just like you, you know, couldn't go anywhere without causing a stir, anyway, you'll see. You might not believe it now, but . . ." She picked up another cat. "You'll end up just like me."

I paid for the wise and wonderful cat lady visit. And then I left, making sure I didn't clip a little kitty tail with the door on my way out.

I fucked lit.
fucked high,
tied up,
in a group,
in public,
on loan,
in a swap.
Fuck her.

*The glass in which the ego seeks to see its face is dark indeed.*
—COURSE IN MIRACLES

"My name is Kim. What's yours?" she Southern-twanged right up to me. She heart pricked me—soft face, dew-blue eyes, *dancered* me.

I had barely worked two years with Gus's company in Chicago when she persuaded me to join her and find dance work in New York. How did she persuade me? It was her accent, her nose, her smile, her sweet blond hair, eyes that blinked like a Disney princess, skin as soft as love. I had a crush.

Kim was apple pie–eyed, a junior teen pageant winner, a Southern belle blond with saucy blue peepers and a tiny pug nose. On first glance, I thought she was a soccer player or a gymnast. Her physique was more athletic than graceful, and she looked like she could beat the shit out of anything. But her accent handled coy, and her puffy, pink-glossed lips and soft-spoken charm hinted at dainty. She was a delicate wrecking ball.

I moved to Midtown Manhattan and lived with her and another friend of hers in a small studio apartment. I slept underneath Kim's lofted bed in an actual closet, nine floors above Thirty-First Street.

Luigi's, Lynn Simonson, Broadway Dance Center—we trained with the legends. We swiped on eye makeup, slogged on spandex, and raced the early morning NYC grid life to get to ballet and jazz classes on time. *42nd Street, Dreamgirls, Nine, Woman of the Year*—I auditioned for all of them. "How tall are you going to say you are?" I whispered to whomever stood nearest. We numbered in the hundreds, in nude legs and high-cut, neckline-plunging leotards, black heeled character shoes. Dancers left dejected as groups were halved and quartered. Kim and I never went for the same gig. I usually ended up in a final cut, worked over, exhausted, maybe three of us on stage—our hands slipping off of our hips, our smiles fake. "Someone will call you by tomorrow morning," we heard from several rows back in a darkened house.

I got a job at world-famous Studio 54. I was a Studio 54 go-go girl, for fuck sake. The lines to get in snaked over long pissed-on, liquored-on sidewalks for blocks, every night of the week. If you were fast, sexy, or cash heavy, the bouncers might cut you in. I'd show up for work in the afternoon while the cleaners were still scrubbing the stench and liquor slop from the previous night's debauchery. On their knees, they scoured the dance floor where likely someone had puked, passed out, or cum. Slunked in the back corner of the bar, hazy young punks were hunting down smokes or snorts before finally heaving themselves out the door. "Get the fuck out of here, scums," they might have heard on their way out, and I felt bad for them. *Go home*, I prayed.

I was go-go on a box. It was the eighties: sequined tops and lamé bell-bottoms, scarves and platform boots and wide elastic belts. I never remembered the lyrics of the songs the DJ played, but I knew the riffs and rhythms, bass lines, and backbeats. Some nights they moved me from the go-go box to the catwalks upstairs. Over the guests dancing below, I curled my flesh into candy cane twists, knotted my body into pretzel bows. I glittered in bras and shiny shorts. The disco balls turned slowly. Marvin Gaye. Donna Summer. "Sexual Healing."

I kept that rhythm walking home in that dirty city. A mile and change, thirty minutes to the studio apartment, Kim and I hoofed it; we both worked there. Donna revved us past the street souls, pods of diminished hope. I wanted to know them, I really did. I'd pass dollar bills into dried-up cupped hands, coffee, smokes, tried to catch an eyeful exchange, but I kept on walking over the piss and stench rising from the subway grates, the whooshed heat up my legs.

Every day, I got high, *sniff snow dust flake*, "feeling the love" deep into my skull, behind my upper lip, brain blitzed and torched. I sucked and snorted in tight corners; nightclub bodies slid against mine. Hopped taxis to the Roxy and late-night skating, followed zombies into underground holes, neon lights, and hidden rooms. Stiff men winking, lost girls in the dark, my hip, my hand brushing against whomever, whatever seemed promising.

One time in a warm underground, a crowded nightspot, I was wasted. He pulled me out the door to a taxi, big khaki jacket. He slid onto the seat, pulling me in alongside him. I wanted sleep. I wanted to get home. I wanted sleep. His hair was thin, a comb-over bald. His khaki jacket was soft, worn, and bunchy like a blanket. His musty beer breath, craggy smoke breath, slipped up my nose. I blacked out. His fat belly woke me, his watery eyes, brown front teeth. He slid his finger under my top lip, swiped right across my gum in the cab, purred in Spanish, more dope. I was twenty.

The stairwell was long and dark, dirty staircase going up; it was an apartment building I realized, and it kept going up. He pushed me through the doorway, closed the door behind us, and then slid the door chain across. Tugging and struggling, he flipped off his belt. We fucked on his floor, in front of the chained door. His pants around his ankles, his ass pumped up and down underneath me; I rode his hairy fat belly. I can't remember when I realized I was on top of him, that I was fucking him on top. Sexual healing. That was the first time I'd ever ridden on top. And old man, grandpa-man, came. He moaned and groaned and curled Spanish before he collapsed underneath me. He purred and slept. I stayed on top of him, spinning, just beyond that chained door, on the filthy floor that smelled of rat poison and smoke and soured single malt. And then I passed out.

The next morning after one last look, I quietly shut the door behind me. I left him snoring on his back, on the floor, with his pants around his ankles where he had pulled them down the night before. I heard the chain swishing against the door on the inside when I pulled it shut. I just kept hearing that chain swishing, swishing, like time stopping, like time not stopping, like tick-tocking and "Wake the fuck up, Tuni"-swishing. I was in Brooklyn. And I was still fucked up. I found the subway and rode it home.

I was glad my roommates were asleep. I pressed the bathroom door closed and turned the shower on hot. Head down, stripped down, I let the water spill on top of me; I smelled old-man cum drain from my cunt.

In the mirror, I stared at the fallen face, drug pocked, scabbed, and swollen. *I think I fucked my father*, I thought as I switched the bathroom light off, bent down, got on my knees, and stuck my finger down my throat. And then I packed my bag.

There were used Trojans all over the sidewalk outside that apartment building door. I hailed a cab to the airport and bought a one-way ticket to Minnesota—followed up that night of Brooklyn with a night in my own childhood bed.

*Taking control of one's narrative repeatedly leads to greater control over memories themselves, making them less intrusive and giving them the kind of meaning that permits them to be integrated into the rest of life.*

—SUSAN BRISON

"I want to go to therapy," I said to my parents a few days later. They were lying in their bed, hadn't gotten up for the day yet. The room was dark; they couldn't see me. "I want the three of us to go to therapy," I said, fucking terrified. Later that afternoon my mother found me in my bedroom doing nothing. Turning my bedroom light on, she said, "I've called an old friend. She will see us tomorrow at two," and walked out.

We drove separately to the counseling appointment, my mother, my father, and I. The psychiatrist's name was Dr. Hall. My mother had seen her before, I think, with one of my siblings, so she knew our family; she had an inkling of who we were. We sat in three simple armed chairs, tic-tac-toe, three idiots in a row, a semi-circle in front of a beige sofa that remained empty. Dr. Hall sat slightly back from the circle like a playground's patrolman, eyes on everyone at once, for safety. I sat between my parents, all of us silent, our eyes non-contacting. I kept my hands and fingers interlaced on my lap.

My brain left the building. Words spun frantically inside my skull: *Look at me! Look at me!* They lifted their heads. The doctor had walked in. Their eyelids opened, and they looked at her as she took her seat outside the circle, straightened her skirt after setting her papers down, and cleared her throat. She looked at each of us one by one. "Well!" she said. And I felt sour and sick; my body jerked and began to tic, jolt, and twitch. I forced a shaky inhale and pushed my shoulders down, lowered my head. I rocked in a tiny circle, like a boat anchored on the sea.

"Hello," she continued. "This will very well be," she spoke slowly, "a challenging forty-five minutes, likely for all of us, and I think to begin with I would like to lay out some ground rules." And then our heads hung again, heavy and lifeless in nooses, a team of rigid anguish. I had assumed my parents felt as I had: boneless, headless, afraid, agonized, or maybe I just hoped they were the same as me. "Listening to each other is very important, without interruptions," she continued, preparing our way through awkward, ugly shame and betrayal. "We will take turns," she went on and gestured with her arms, explaining that she held "tragedy" in one hand and "forgiveness" in the other. "We all have weaknesses," she said slowly, opening her right hand in offering, "and courage," and copied the movement with her left. "We have vulnerabilities and we have love." *She believes me, do you hear her, she believes me*, my brain was flailing.

"Can you remember what Tuni has described for us?" she asked, turning toward my father, to me, to my mother, easing us, steering us carefully back into my bedroom. He sat to my right with his legs uncrossed, stiffly, in dress shoes. His drifting wet eyes met mine like a hiccup, a dart to a bullseye, and then he looked away. I felt it, no words, just his eye blip, a Morse-coded apology? *Say it, Dad! Say it!* His eyes were filling, then dripping. He shifted his mouth—it was as if his lips started to shape a word, and I thought he was about to say something, and then a hiccup again and no words came out, and he closed his mouth and he swallowed. His Adam's apple bobbed, his feet shifted, he fell silent. He pulled his bottom lip under the top lip, grimaced, inhaled until his lips flared like a brisk wind had just blasted across his face, a flash of his darkened coffee teeth, wine teeth. He re-pursed, returned his gaze to his dress shoes, raven black and shiny.

"I told him not to," I thought I heard my mother whisper behind me—to the back of my head, I swore it—so I turned to face her, to confirm what I thought she had just said. *You told him not to? What did you say?* The words spun in front of my eyes, but I couldn't get them out; her face was blank. She had nothing to say. *I hate you,* I thought before swimming away.

"I believe you said you were at the doorway . . ." Dr. Hall moderated, offering again with her right hand open, "Danger," and again in her left hand, "Remorse?" "Forgiveness?" But there was that sharp catch in my mother's breath. She gasped or was she choking? No. No, she would not choke. She hitched her chair a little closer to Dr. Hall's, a little farther away from me.

"I never saw," she said coldly and turned her whole body to face mine, a pivot, and set her hand firmly on my arm, widening her eyes, the eyes of a black crow, "I didn't see anything," she cawed, flapping her wings.

But I remembered. As she sat with her whole body facing mine, next to Dr. Hall, I remembered her silhouette there in my bedroom, her lean onto my bedroom doorframe, half of her body, half of her face turned inward into the wood, a mommy's cubist profile, rib cage, hip, knee, foot, never in, never out. Or maybe it was he who made her look so angular, my father distorting her shadow at the door as he stood tall next to me, me in bed, him boxing her body out. *Can you see me? Mama?* I remembered seeing her, my thighs squirmy, my butt pinching. *Mommy!*

# dream two

*In a dream, I am peacocking a drum major's strut, and I'm teasing passengers in a Greyhound bus parked alongside me. Then suddenly I slip on ice and flail comically as though on skates, arms and legs windmilling toward a wipeout until, thank God, I once again find balance. I pump my bicep like Popeye, spinach and cheese, and wink toward the windows of the bus, everyone staring, their expressions transitioning from aghast to amazed.* Ha ha, *I think to myself.* I have done it again *and begin to high-knee march and swing my arms with cocky delight. I step in front of the bus as though to lead it when suddenly the bus driver, unaware I am in front of him, rolls out, rolls the bus forward and flattens me. The long bus driving on, years and years of its undercarriage pressing my insides into air, into nothingness.*

*By the time my family has found me, I am a cardboard corpse, recognizable features, clothing and shape preserved, but paper-thin and dead. Except I hear them, screaming and wailing and phoning 911 and grieving and dancing; they are dancing to heighten their grief, which livens me, and without them seeing, I begin to re-fill—slowly but fully—and return to a three-dimensional puffed-out-like-a-porn-doll-human and stand a little wobbly and say, "Well, this will be a little more challenging than I thought," before the EMTs arrive and lift me carefully away.*

What was my father thinking? Why wouldn't my mother tell her? I kept looking at Dr. Hall, not knowing what more to do. And I guess Dr. Hall didn't know what more to do either. By the end of the hour, she conjured a to-do list, assignments for the three of us to consider, "in order to continue the conversation you've started," she hoped.

My father's silence I more or less expected. But my mother's cold curse, her stare, her bird eyes wide and dry, the way she banished the hand of regret or error or fault—that I hadn't planned for. My father looked at me once more when he stood, stood tall on the black shining shoes. Our session had finished, and the dead silence had gone on long enough; he was deflated, skeletal. All of us, I thought, were made of mistakes, trials and errors, mistakes that buried love. I did believe he was silently reckoning with his. I would forgive him.

There would be no second session. I left Dr. Hall's office that day, walked back to my car, and never spoke to them about it again.

Later, my mother told me she had never loved her mother. Later, she told me she regretted she hadn't given her father the love he deserved. Was she wanting me to know how she suffered? More than I? Was she wanting me to know how she had never been seen or heard by her parents? Maybe, I thought, she was afraid I would not love her just as she had ended up not loving her mother, and that's why she couldn't tell me the truth. And maybe she thought that no one would believe me, so in the end, I would have to love her.

"Your father knows a very good doctor." My mother paused. "He will make you feel better about yourself." And I remember my shoulders tensing and untensing. I remember my eyes closing, understanding that up to that point in my life, I was a self-perpetuating failure, a quitter. I was unable to grasp the techniques of long-term planning. I lacked speech. I couldn't stand behind an opinion. I was unable to *un-fake* my existence. After that therapy session, I maintained a tiptoe in their home, afraid. "I have already contacted him," she went on, "and you can see him as soon as tomorrow. I'll take you."

I was *grossly underweight*. New York had been an eighteen-month cocaine-driven sexcapade. I had escorted my promising and phenomenally skilled body down the literal toilet. "I'll take you," she said again, "and you'll be perfect." My breasts were as small as buttercups, a whiskey shot thrown back. My breasts were as small as the spit of whiskey backwash in a glass. And that was distasteful to my mother. "It's just what you need. I think. Don't you?" Clearly. I was in need of one more thing that would enhance my sexual identity.

My mother brought me to the doctor's office. I sat in the paper dress and waited for the doctor to come in while the one person in the world who's supposed to love me as I am, no matter what, held up silhouettes of B, C, D, and E cups, drawn in black on a white background, a laminated chart. "I guess B?" I shrugged at her.

"C," she replied. "Or maybe you want to be a D, like me." She winked. My mother was a Jayne Mansfield, a bunny dream.

"Are you sure?" the doctor repeated one more time. I looked at my mother; she nodded yes. I nodded yes.

I got big breasts, a pair of big, hard, rock melons on my malnourished, waif body. Following the surgery, I recalibrated my self-perception from lithe to thick. While bandaged and healing, I lay on the floor of my bedroom in my parents' house, stomach down, nose to wood, and rocked, painfully, over the mound on my left side, port-side, before a slow seesaw rock to my right side, starboard, back and forth on the silicone sea, flattening the brand-new breasts. I was a sinking ship. But I got my old job back, I returned to Chicago, and the company I had left two years before, a peek a betty boo-boo, brand-new girl.

"I'm a late bloomer," I lied again and again when asked about them, back in rehearsals. "Are those real?"

"Yes," I'd whisper, disgusted, fully fake. No one cared. I knew I fooled no one, but couldn't admit the truth. I would have been pitied and dismissed.

From the outset, I wanted a do-over, and wished I'd said *no*. I knocked them down by doubling up on extra-small sports bras, concealed them under oversized sweatshirts. After weekly weigh-ins, my coach predictably lifted an eyebrow, insisting a pound or two lost would be helpful to streamline my shape. I had no more fat to give. My bountiful boulders were stared at and doubled the number of whistling clowns, inspired invitations to climb poles, strip for photos, catch rides. I was now the physical spit of my mother.

# a letter to tuni from tuni:

Dearest t,

Yo. Let's take a break, can we? Can we talk about scars for a second, mama?

Do you remember that time—you must've been four—and you were in kindergarten? You were coming home from school in that taxicab, and somehow your winter coat got caught in the passenger door as you were climbing out and wham, right? You slammed it, but you didn't know your coat was caught (I mean, you were four) and neither did that cab driver (I mean, what are the odds—whoops) and off he went. That postman saved you. He ran right into the street and blocked that cab with his body. "Good thing it was winter," your mother used to say in the retelling. "She only burned out her knees, ankles, wrists, and chin," and she counted off your body parts with her fingers. Those scars weren't that bad.

*Or that time at your parents' house when you were in high school and for some reason you decided to use a pressure cooker to make popcorn. It was like a dinosaur pot, heavy as a kettle bell but big enough to make a huge batch, which was what you wanted. You poured in the kernels and fastened the lid, and when it was done—super smart with that oven mitt on your right hand—you grabbed the handle with your* left *hand (dumbass). And that fucker pot was balls heavy, and since you were about to drop it (cuz you're not left-handed), you pulled your right arm underneath the cooker for balance, to prop it, and you slow-sizzled your forearm like hamburger beef. Yikes. That inkblot scar reminded you for an exceptionally long time how fucking stupid you were.*

*Course, you had, you know, the knee surgeries, whatever, fingers, thumbs—all the types of life's surgical bullshits. But the scars at your breasts, the wide secret smiles under each one, those jokers' grins, those fucked you up, didn't they? Those kept you dark and small and, yep, fake, fake, fake, fake, fake. You called them bad wrinkles, right? Ha! You said, "What scars? Those are scratches, biopsies, birthmarks, wear and tear." You didn't, wouldn't, couldn't admit you had fake tits. Lovers didn't need to know; husbands didn't ask (did you really think they couldn't tell?). You were like a beautiful little butterfly in a diving bell; you were a self-made, locked-in, locked-up liar. And you lost your hug too. That was the kicker. You fucking gave up the hug. You pulled away from the people who wanted to greet you for real, the ones who tried loving you or supporting you, the ones who wanted to congratulate you. You pulled your heart away from them because you were so ashamed, and as you leaned in with your cheek you left a mountain of space between your tits and their touch. There was no other way to hide your fraud.*

*But of course, hilarious, with all of the effort you undertook to hide the truth, no one was fooled. So that sanctuary, that make-believe escape hatch ocean of graceful lines and spins and body curls and shapes that, oh yeah, others envied, that place that saved you when you were little—yeah, I get it. It was now a sinkhole. Instead of the vast and mighty ocean, you were the diving bell, the only place you could take a full breath, the only place you could let your guard down, the only place you could stop the perfect. Alone. Enchambered.*

*But honestly, it was the accident that kind of woke you the fuck up. I mean, you'd been through some stuff by then, and you did fine, but the accident was the final straw. You were blindsided and in pieces. I know it was just your arms, but your arms were toast. You couldn't eat, clean yourself, hold a book, wipe your ass. Thank God you insisted on the bidet. But you couldn't turn over in bed or lean one way or another to even get up out of the bed—a straitjacket. And if you got on your feet, you were terrified, like heart-splitting horrified you would get knocked right back down, pushed by a dog, not see what was coming from around a corner and break humpty-dumpty style all over again.*

*Plus, the opiates, I mean whoa, the Percocets and hydrocodones and oxycodones—you were fucked up on the drugs from morning until night, spinning, thick, slow, detached. You became obsessed with Steve Harvey, oh my God, remember? Around-the-clock* Family Feud, *Steve Harvey and that incredibly gorgeous smile, those phenomenal white teeth, fucking gorgeous, funniest man alive. When you changed rooms, someone had to get him on the other TV in the next room, because, lifeline, am I right? You found "Smelly Cat" that summer too, fucking Phoebe and Chandler.*

*But you finally and wholly unhinged. You couldn't tolerate la-la land any longer, and you quit cold turkey. Ugh. You remember. Your arm was a fire torch, a blood-boiling burning torch attached at your shoulder. You screamed, you flailed, you thrashed. You foamed at the mouth.*

*But miraculously, your best friend happened to call you, thank God, right in that moment, right when you wanted nothing but death, you screamed, "I can't do this!" and she was ringing you, and that phone, somehow, was right next to your fingers* (miracle) *and you pressed go, because deep down you knew if there was anyone that would be able to help you, it was her.*

*She saved your sorry ass. And that scar healed up great, it really did, like a thin stream running from your wrist to your shoulder, sealed, at least for a little while, I know. And you got off the boogie man shit, eventually. You did good, kid.*

"Trauma begets the road to freedom, [and]crises generate epiphanies." *You remember when you read that? Mmm-hmmm, Gail Sheehy, in her book Passages. You loved that book and you had one of those "a-ha" moments when you read that. I mean, I don't think you actually believed you suffered trauma as a little girl, like that was what happened to other little girls, not to you. You did not put those two together. But you totally got the concept; it made perfect sense to you, right? And then after the accident, BAM. You saw trauma everywhere! Your father and your mother, for fucking sure—trauma. Your husband, your ex-husbands—everywhere you turned you knew there were stories to be uncovered, fears, suffering— trauma was fucking all over the place, Buddha. And I think that's when you decided "enough," decided that you could imagine the love overtaking the ego shit, that dumb ego bullshit, and you thought yup, swap love for ego.*

*So in that instance, the diving bell helped you; it actually enabled you to tear down your walls instead of hiding behind them. Scars, yup. Healing, yup. Shit happens, yup. Egos suck, yup, yup. Love is the revolution.*

Stella, my former ballet mistress, said, "Well, look who's back," as I situated myself at the barre. She was small. Her dyed brown hair extended from her natural white roots and into a proper bun, tight and twisted at the back of her head.

There were small chunks of rosin gold piled at the floor's baseboard to my left, flecks of it on the tops of my slippers and more pressed into my heels. Flaying my inner thighs apart, while pressing my tail down underneath me toward the floor, my diamond descended from first position, a demi plié. I rotated at the tops of my thigh bones; I turned the bones into my pelvis. I lengthened my toes along the floor and shifted the weight of my body minutely to the left. My spine stretched upward as my right arm lifted. A veil. Ports de bras. Some of the most beautiful lines of ballet, of dance in general, are magnified and connected to the sublime holiness of the arms.

My arm reversed, returned, and lowered as I descended into plié again, my pinky finger feather-brushed the top of my knee. After the plié, I folded my torso forward over my legs before stretching out and up and out and waterfalling backward into the opposite arc. "You're behind count," Stella snapped. "Keep up." Her eyes pierced my torso; my breasts were late, too slow.

I lit up after class on the rooftop, guzzled Mountain Dew, lit up another off the first. Popped Sudafed. Crushed a NoDoz and snorted it before my next class. I was so ashamed.

Somehow, some way, grace happened. I had purchased a last-minute ticket to see the Joseph Holmes Dance Theatre perform just down the street from Gus's studio. The auditorium was full. In the last row of the main floor section of the house, I squeezed between the slacked and skirted knees to my seat in the middle of the row. The lights lowered. The curtains lifted. And the JHDT dancers transformed the energy of the room; the atmosphere of the theater embodied holy spirit—prayerful, worshipful dance. I saw them as divine lights, like messengers of winged gospel revealing a diorama of African American culture, shimmying, snapping, soulful glory.

I had performed roles choreographed by Chicago legends, jazz dance pioneers who helped put jazz dance into the history books. But Randy's company, JHDT, was something different. It was a faith aesthetic, inspired by devotion and charity, performed as a brother and sisterhood. I began immediately taking classes at their studio, stood side by side with them at their ballet barre, and a few weeks later, Randy hired me. He couldn't have known he had gifted me a sacred restart. I felt I was participating in something larger than myself, that I was being offered an opportunity to convey universal beauty from within.

JHDT's dance studio was a thumbprint, a tiny, framed sweatbox above a rundown convenience store in the heart of "Boystown," Chicago. After joining the company, I moved a hundred footsteps away from it on Pine Grove Avenue, into an unremarkable fifteen-story redbrick apartment building. I slept on a framed futon next to two thrift store chairs and a coffee table on which sat my hefty Budweiser ashtray, predictably overfilled with pink lippy–stained butts of Marlboro Lights.

I was experiencing over and over again that dance was the only way I could authentically express myself. I tried teaching dance at one point during that time, kids in the suburbs, adults at fitness clubs. I tried to find the words to convey how I wanted them to move and to explain to them how to experience what I experienced, but I couldn't translate into words what I intuitively did, experienced, knew. I tried to get students to witness the unity, the release, the unbound joy of connecting to their bodies and to transport that connection from the studio into their daily lives. I failed.

One day I was learning a piece in class, a mash-up of animalistic and lyrical moves, fiercely athletic, electric fast. We lined up in the back corner of the room and waited for our turns to explode two by two, dancing to the catty corner.

My turn. A body roll, I slid into an arabesque balance that fell into an offshoot, off-balanced suspension; a layout, I dropped down to the floor and spun, rebounded, pushed up, and jumped into leg splits that reached the ceiling. I remembered. I saw myself in the mirror. I was sailing horizontally.

In the mirror, my arched feet curled to their peaks, my legs daggered the walls of the room east and west. I was weightless, hovering, wide open. Deep Forest *World Mix* played, a bohemian ballet, an exotic, indigenously rhythmic composition.

A Marley floor could have a slick spot on its rubber surface. A cold section of the floor might cause a dancer to slip, or a puddle of sweat might do that. I didn't know what happened that day except that my right foot skidded on the landing. My momentum pushed my body along into the next count, but my knee was following my skid in a different direction. I crashed onto the floor grabbing the pop, hearing it snap, and feeling a mechanical implosion of my joint.

The other dancers stopped dancing because I hadn't gotten back up. "No, no . . . I'm okay," I lied, waving them off as they drew in closer. It was a known risk, every day, we all knew it. "I promise, I'm fine. I'll take a break, a minute," I said, looking toward the teacher, knowing I would be replaced.

"Deep Forest," he winked and signaled at the next group in the corner, turned the volume back up. Below the small bench in the lobby were my Steve Madden chunky-heeled Mary Janes. The bohemian ballet pulsed under the studio door as I slipped them on and limped home.

*Now what?* floated in my head that night as my livelihood and my identity vanished. An ice bag drenched my sweats, drenched the cover of my futon, dripped onto the floor. I had no employable skill except the one I had just snapped. I barely had a high school degree. I'd swallowed whatever medication I thought would make it all go away. I drank wine until a brink, until an easy swerve, until a barely managed escape to the kitchen sink, where I had set the glass down, chucked the ice bag, flattened my hand along the hallway wall until I found the floor. *Now what?* looped over and over until blackout.

Self-preservation came to a crashing halt; I didn't know what to do.

*part two-b*

2.0

He was sexy. I met him at a retail store where I had gotten
a job selling tents and climbing gear and sleeping bags—
basically, stuff I knew nothing about. I couldn't get enough
of his scent, his curled puckery smile, his raw vulnerability,
his soft skin. I'd asked him over to my place. He was taking
college courses at night, and I said, "Come over after," and
I waited by the door and I listened to Enya and I listened to
the synthesizers and the sweet and quiet uilleann pipes, her
haunting voice as I waited for him.

My mother tried talking me out of becoming a mother;
she begged me to abort. Her criticisms of me, her persistent
pleas to end at the beginning, had to have been born from her
own unresolved issues, that's what I thought. Or maybe her
unmanaged disappointments? Or lack of self-love? I couldn't
know how she suffered then, because she wasn't telling me,
and I wasn't asking. I would not attempt to unpack her or
try to figure her out.

Paul and I got married in our seventh month of preg-
nancy together in an old Polish banquet hall in the South
Side of Chicago. I wore pale yellow, full-length gloves and
vintage lace-up ivory boots that almost matched my vanilla
minidress. I wore a sheer crinoline stovepipe hat, and my
big baby belly grinned wide across my front. Paul's suit was
a thrift store find. Bone-white slacks and suit jacket, sweet

wide lapels, a violet button-down with a same-colored tie, and two-toned brown-and-white wing tip shoes. We combusted from schnitzel, cabbage rolls, pierogis, meatballs, and kraut; we danced to Polish mazurka music and painted each other in buttercream frosting.

Miracle: I stopped sticking my finger down my throat the minute I discovered I was pregnant. Miracle: I quit smoking that same minute. I enrolled in massage therapy school and studied anatomy and physiology and experienced hands-on cadaver training. Turned out I did not need a stable knee to become a massage therapist or a mama.

Our son was born six weeks premature, and of course he was perfect. He did develop jaundice a few days later, though, which sent him back to the hospital and under the blue lights. My own baby Picasso Blue, his light box bounced rheumy and warm ocean wave shadows along the sterile walls of his room; his tiny trampoline chest fluttered at his sternum. His IV tube was taped onto a small block and attached to his arm. I kept my hand on him, on his cool blue aquarium. I watched my boy from the cot they brought in for me to sleep on and marveled at the miracle of him. I pumped my enormous and heavy breasts, tight with hot motherhood. I squished them into awkwardly sucking, impossibly tiny plastic cones. It spittled. It leaked out of the suction cup and down between my fingers, which made them sticky, stick together. His bitty lips pinched as my thick colostrum landed there. I believed in mother's love. I believed in him.

I missed the memo about getting pregnant while nursing an infant, and right about the time my firstborn was swapping my nipple for his bottle, my doctor informed me baby number two was on her way. In three years, Paul and I established a marriage and became a family of four. In other words, we were asking a lot of each other, from ourselves, and of our little ones.

He was the spit of John Lennon—pale skinned, auburn haired, eyes set close together, long oval shaped face and deep cheeks under prominent cheekbones. His lips twitched into pucker kisses when he spoke. He had an estranged, absent father, which likely contributed to his diminished sense of self-importance. Who escapes the feeling of unbelonging? I don't know of anyone.

Born on the northwest side of Chicago, he high-schooled in the North Center neighborhood, west of Wrigley Field. He rotated in Chicago dogs, White Castles, and Italian beefs. He preferred the short cuts, the backstreets, and alley secrets. His blood pulsed rock and roll, punk, and indie bands. "Who is this?" I asked once errand-running in his Pinto.

"Jane's Addiction," he smiled, swerving around traffic on the road to nowhere, and proceeded to reveal the band's history, the names of every musician, whether or not they played in other bands, who produced them.

We were sex and love backdropped by the Pistols, heavy steins of Hefeweizen, deep-dish pizza pies, and bowling. We were booth photos at the Rainbow Room with my platinum dyed hair and our babies in our arms, baby cheeks pressed against my mod jumper, bubbly toes flexing near his chin. We posed as it flashed every fifteen seconds, my eyes heavily coaled, my lips frosted. Paul's hair buzzed tight. He wore a perfect goatee and thin gold frames. Most likely his T-shirt featured The Who.

Our babies between us, we were dopey and hip and stream of consciousness and carefree and four or five steps ahead of ourselves, kissing babies, kissing each other. Neither of us had anticipated how the vulnerabilities inherent in savage love would stack up, how shepherding miracles would demand a blistery reckoning of who we were. Neither of us.

We began to suffer instead of thriving, and instead of allowing a full collapse, we decided to call a time-out.

*I feared suicide. I never feared for myself, that I would weigh
it as an option. It wasn't an option. It was never an option.
But I had feared losing someone I loved to suicide. When I
lay in bed next to my lover sensing his unrest, I reflexively
inverted, my heart peeled itself from his skin, my blood, my
bones, filled with fear, and I turned away from devotion
toward fearful uncertainty. And then, I would have touched
something—a shoulder, his. And I would have squeezed him
until my heartbeat returned, calmer, softer, and my fear and
my tension dissipated, and I could begin again. But it cycled
back, and my uncertainty surged. I struggled when trying to
respond appropriately to another's desperations. I struggled
to understand my loved one's mania and depression; I was
frightened and helpless. And I became someone who, when
overwhelmed with fear, doubted my ability to stand for him,
stand up for him. I fled.*

    *I ran from friends and their demons too. Maybe because
it looked too familiar? I believed I had only enough stored
salvation inside for me. I didn't want to be the one lack-
ing courage, who remained silent, and who could sever love
because of fear. But I did do that. In the face of someone*

*I loved becoming undone, I turned away, cowardly. I put myself first and moved on, thus denying the possibility of love's guidance. I grabbed a child in each of my hands and ran. **And for this, I plead for forgiveness.** I was so afraid.*

*I am not saying if I had made different choices, everything would have been Cracker Jacks and baseball.*

*I am not saying I am not allowed to make mistakes and fail. I am not saying if I could do it all over again, I would do it differently.*

*But if asked, "Why should I live? What is so great about staying alive?" I'd have said, "Digging hands and fingernails into dry, cool dirt can soothe restlessness. Palming seeds and letting them fall into tilled soil and allowing for the expansion of life, experiencing nature's journey, could guide you toward the divine. Sitting riverside, or better, sitting aside the awe-giving ocean with rippling sheets of iced and foamed wet cold cascading onto hot, dry sand, with whipping winds slap-stinging the skin of your face in an instant is a YES; it is an invitation for worship."*

*"What is so great about staying alive?" I'd continue, "Moss—edible, expansive, encompassing all of the earth in its cape.*

*"Seeing and being seen, the tenderness inside the hearts of those you connect with, inviting them to layer their sacred onto your sacred, glances and steps toward one another, breaking away and making space, making peace within grief, within heartbreak, within joy—their air, your breath, love."*

*I may not have understood how you felt, not the depth of despair you might have been enduring night after day after night, but that wasn't because I didn't want to. I needed your help, and I should have said so. I should have asked. I needed your help.*

*Please accept my apology—for not doing enough, for not standing still, standing up for you.*

*Stay.*

*Perhaps one did not want to be loved so much as to be understood.*

—GEORGE ORWELL

I fled. I didn't want to understand. I couldn't take myself apart in the way necessary to feel what he was feeling. That would have entailed me feeling and me losing control. Our firstborn was not yet two years old, and our second born was nine months. I was mama.

"I think I have a gig this Friday. Would there be any way you can take them Friday night instead of Saturday morning?"

"Well, I'll have to let you know tomorrow. Is that okay? I might have something."

Or "Can I please have them on Thanksgiving?"

"Well, my mom hasn't seen them in a while, and she told me she really wants the kids for Thanksgiving dinner." He always sounded as though he regretted the excuses he made when he said no.

At the same time, and gratefully, my children were not asking, "Mommy, why aren't you and Daddy living in the same house?" Yet. My oldest was barely using words; my youngest was far from them. I found myself listening to what others said to console me: "They'll never remember the two of you together."

"It would be so much harder if they were older, in middle school or high school."

"Kids are so resilient."

"Kids are happier when their parents are happier; being raised by parents who aren't in love would be far worse." My ass. And we were in love. There wasn't a single rule or slice of advice that held up when we tried to navigate our two households with our one divided family. There was not a way to cup innocent heartbeats through chaos without the sadness and anger seeping into their bloodstreams.

Eventually, I rented a one-bedroom apartment, slid a crib into one corner and a child's bed into the other. I slept on the pullout sofa. I painted the apartment walls yellow and accented them with a whimsical red-lettered alphabet. We ate a lot of Happy Meals. I was thirty years old, not quite dancing with single motherhood. But before that, before I'd really cut the ties, I had moved in with Emmy.

A friend of mine, Jeron, had told me about Emmy many years before I was married. He had said she wanted to be my friend, but she thought I was such a bitch. "I explained to her you're actually really nice," Jeron said. "I don't know why she's so hung up on making you out that way, but I swear if you two got to know each other, you'd be besties for sure!"

So I said, "Of course, introduce us!" I knew who she was. I'd seen her in dance classes.

"Who knows," he shrugged. "Maybe she's just intimidated by you." He winked. I had heard that a lot. I knew I was a handful, but I also thought my insecurities and lack of self-esteem were plain to see.

She was almost a white blond, with hair so fine she was nymphlike. She was a canopy of moss, a pale mushroom, a bursting acorn. She hiccupped and giggled and sang as she breathed. She harrumphed like Pooh Bear and snorted backwards, rolling *rrr*'s as she laughed. Down the road, it was what we did most often together; we knitted laughter. We thieved happy mischief. Her skin was milkweed pink flushed over farm girl Iowa-born cream. She was modern dance to my ballet jazz. But the ways in which we styled ourselves, our thrift store wardrobes of crazy put-togethers braided us tightly: her violet suede fringed jacket echoed her fringed white hair brushing secrets off her shoulders, T-shirts and seafoam short shorts while roller-skating in our kitchen. Me in sheer cotton jackets with ruffles and ties and cutoff jean shorts and thigh-high black boots, dancing and smoking and watching her skate. Roxy music and Nine Inch Nails backdropped our candlelit meals we shared at our thrifted kitchen table. And together for a decade, with her cat, we became a family, each other's mother, secret holder, laundry folder. "Come closer," she said, her fairy puffed hair, her pale eyes wanting.

"I'm here," I said. We were so close.

On my left was where she stood when I married. At the foot of the bed was where she stood when I delivered my firstborn, cooing and nuzzling him within moments of his arrival on earth. Jeron was right. We became best friends.

I packed a bag for me and the kids, left Paul, and stayed with Emmy in her apartment, a short-term solution with the hope that Paul and I would figure out our shit. It was a big ask, taking us all into her place. The longer I slept away, though, the steadier I began to feel, and instead of rushing back to him, I found an apartment for the three of us, scrambled a new home together. Was it then I shipwrecked his trust? Was that the minute we capsized? I was back at me first, saving myself, sailing away. In ways I hadn't anticipated or imagined, I was redoing my childhood and hoping beyond anything to create a safe and protective haven for the three of us; I thought it might lead to us being a foursome again.

Sometimes Emmy pinch-hit as mama-babysitter, or we teamed them, dressed them in oversized basketball shorts that kissed their anklebones or threw thrift store hoodies on them, hems below their knees, before marching to the playground, fastening them into swings, racing them up and down the steel slides. We squealed ourselves all over them. I relied so heavily on her. But fuck. Paul did too.

That morning.

That morning.

That morning I saw her stepping out of Paul's apartment. That morning, I had parked. I'd arrived a few minutes early with the kids, and it was Paul's turn; it was Paul's day with our babies.

And that morning, there was Emmy, running out of my old side door, purple fringe suede jacket, secrets, secrets.

I turned the car off and rubbed my eyes. *It couldn't be*, I quickly prayed, *but of course it was*, terror laughed and sliced me open, exposing all of me. Terror did the exact same thing when my mom died years later. On first awareness, finding my mother, I'd lost it all: words, form, breath, time, heartbeat, and then terror arrived and splayed me crazy.

My babies waited in their seats behind me. I was holding my breath and silently screaming. My fingers shook pulling up the lock of the door. I became a steam engine, steam, a fireball. I was anarchy.

That morning, I opened the car door; I found the curb, the sidewalk. Emmy in her purple fringe suede jacket, the one I had borrowed so many times, the one I had consistently begged to wear, and I knew she loved that I loved it so much, that I'd wanted to be like her.

Emmy running to her car parked alongside my old apartment building, the same spot I had liked to park in too, because it was nearer the side door, the door she came out of.

Emmy running.

The street short-circuited, and my knees burned like fire and slid sideways, and my stomach lurched and twisted and disintegrated as I stumbled around the back of the car, and my babies watched and waited from inside, the back seat, in their car seats, Goldfish cracker crumbs under their bums, soggy spots where the juice boxes spilled out, where the sippy cups always became wedged.

*What am I supposed to do?*

My babies stared, began to squirm and reach for me from inside the car, but I couldn't. I didn't know what to do. I turned my back to them, crying, tears flying out of my eyes. "Emmy!" I wailed, screamed, wailed, wept. She pulled her car from the parking space and made a U-turn. She pulled away.

"Emmy!"

Terror opened the car door and somehow unbuckled the babies.

Despair held one on her hip and gripped the hand of the other.

Anarchy had already hitched their overnight bag over her shoulder.

Mania crossed them over the street and accompanied them up the two staircases to their old apartment door.

Fear waited as Paul opened the door for no one's eyes to meet while the babies hugged daddy legs and spun off into toys and daddy-ville. And I hiccupped and choked and snorted and held tragedy's hand back down the stairs, calling up as I left, "Please have them home tomorrow by dinner." Wondering how I'd managed words from my mouth, wondering who was speaking.

I was back in my apartment, somehow, thirty minutes later, trying to decide how big a cardboard box I would need to shit in, to actually squat over and take a massive shit in, tape it up, seal it in, and leave it on Emmy's doorstep. And that was all I thought about for years. I thought of Emmy;

I thought of shitting in a box. I should have. That was the only thing I thought of to do.

Where I thought I was going from the moment I saw her running down the sidewalk took a sharp and never-go-back turn into tailspin. I didn't blame Paul. I never did. I knew he was hurting, and he needed help. I guess I could have blamed him, but just like navigating my mother and father, I could forgive Paul more easily, just like I had my dad. I felt the most betrayed by my best friend. I felt the most betrayed by the woman who stood next to me when I got married. I felt the most betrayed by the woman who helped me welcome my firstborn son to the world. I felt most betrayed by the first woman to teach me sister friendship. I felt most betrayed by the woman who I thought had my back.

**Turn around, Emmy.**

**Emmy, turn around.**

Over fifteen years would pass before I ever saw Emmy again. She appeared at my eldest's high school basketball game one Friday night with Paul. I arrived excited as usual to see my boy play, and then there they were standing in the gym lobby together, standing shoulder to shoulder waiting, it appeared, their backs to the entrance of the gym, their fronts to the main doors I had just walked through. They looked scared. Nervous. Were they hopeful? Were they in love? My hands fell off my wrists. My shoulder joints, my hip and knee joints dissolved; the walls of my heart inverted and bled.

I sat behind them in the bleachers, two rows up, a mountain, a glacial peak, a lifetime's switchback away from her, her fine blond wisps catching her jawline, resting on her pale milky skin.

They had recently reunited, my daughter told me the next day. They were engaged, she continued.

And they married the following summer.

Guiding minds without being able to read minds was hard. I was keenly aware that I was learning how to be a mother on the fly, and solo. But I didn't realize how much I depended on them for instruction—they were only two years old and one year old—they didn't have much by way of offering me hints that I could easily comprehend. So I riffed, a lot, and falling short of my babies' needs was an excruciating heartache. I knew I had created a challenging situation for them, and I naively thought my love would mitigate the hardships that come with being a child of two people who are no longer together, no longer a love team, no longer living under the same rooftop, no longer offering a unified force against enemies and fears and doubts and night terrors. I had inadvertently created a hardship I could only stumble-navigate. I didn't see how I had eroded their trust, how I had changed the rules of their road, invited confusion into every day, and unraveled their nest. We were all on the edge of that switchback, off-balance, relying on instincts—and entirely because I was naming my survival. My name: muddied, sullied, betrayed, abused, worn, hurt, afraid but enduring with an oak's resilience, persisting with an ocean's might, bearing a daughter's courage. My parents were out of state and showed no interest in helping me. And I was too proud to ask for help. I hadn't figured out true compassion, for if I had, if I had slowed my steps away from Paul, I would have been kinder to him, I would have crossed over and joined his fears.

"Let's get your jammies on," I begged my whirling dervishes, bumping and giggling into each other, the furniture, me. I chased them until we danced. They jumped over the discarded action figures and landed headlong onto the sofa's pile of books. The nightly routine was a landing strip, ours for dismissing the to-dos of daytime: the day care check-ins and the passing off of crackers and fruits, wipes and diapers, changes of clothing. I trusted the *village* because I had to. The day care staff had eyes on them, kept them safe, encouraged, nurtured, and disciplined them so I could work. It was in daycare that *ketchup on rice became a phenomenon, more delicious and pined for than chocolate milk.

I lived north and worked south. Our commute into the city to the day care became a cherished and protected time together, mindful, and complete—singing, laughing, learning. "I dreamt about meatballs raining from heaven," my little man shouted, strapped in, his eyes widening beyond his grin. "I built a meatball tower and surrounded the dragons, but then they opened their mouths and cooked the meat with their fire and ate it!" Next to him, baby mama pounded the passenger seat in front of her, and in rhythm I bounced as she accentuated her brother's storytelling with her buckled shoes, a sippy cup in her mouth, spit and bubbles.

"Let's get your jammies on," I repeated that night. The tiny metal tag in between my fingers, I zipped my creatures into their sleepers, pulled the fleeced fabric away from their relaxed and bulging toddlery tums. She in her raggedy worn Cinderella suit, powder-blue eyes with a sparkly future, and he in a Donatello he loved, the brainy, inventor Ninja Turtle in mid-flight. "Let's get your jammies on!" A celebration. I caught my spiraling children in my hands one by one, lifted them up, over and over. I held them overhead, babies in my arms, babies filling me up, tossing them and catching them. We were starting over, forming new rhythms, becoming a new dance. What was not lost on me was that our new home was only blocks from where I had first landed after graduating high school, fifteen years before then, with Charlene and Michael and Kenny and Jeffrey, and when dance was my entire universe.

I had a gig in downtown Chicago one night, and as I was getting myself ready in the bathroom I could see them in the reflection of the mirror. The doorway to their bedroom and their silhouettes in the glass—they were pacing while they brushed their teeth, eyeing each other, messaging sibling secrets, and dribbling white foamy goop onto their chins and onto their sleepers. I was fanning eyelash glue over the bathroom sink as I watched them, wishing I could undress for bed instead. The babysitter was due. *I will ask her to tuck them in too*, I thought to myself. I didn't want them to wake up after I left and be surprised by someone they didn't know. I hated my reliance on agencies, paying someone to sweeten their dreams.

I needed these evening gigs, and for the most part I rationalized my absence from my babies by reminding myself they would be asleep for most of the time I was gone. These jobs paid well. Sometimes it was a go-go box; other times it was an illusion of my body being sawed in half, transformed into a tiger, a magician's illusions I'd sworn to keep secret. My knee wasn't stable, but I could always maneuver around a wizard's sleight of hand.

It almost always happened like it had the week before: a heavy hand on my waist, firmly pressing in and pinching, fingers above my hip bone, thumb at the small of my back.

Walking toward the restroom just outside the ballroom for a costume change, I tensed. Someone pulled me back as the waitstaff stepped around me, serving guests their meals. The room moved quickly, and I turned to face him. I doubt he knew the mistake he'd made—he had a glazed look that sized me over, like he was admiring a Corvette. He couldn't have known I was no Corvette. I was a bitch on wheels. Glasses clinked, laughter. Scents of beef and rosemary, his heavy cologne, spicy and rude.

He was sloppy. He kept pressuring my waist. What he didn't know was my performance onstage fusing free-falling sensuality into space was not for his pleasure but my own. It was how I stayed afloat, how I moved on from the past, and it was as natural to me as a survival technique needed to be, like breath. He pulled and squeezed again; his sweaty liquored breath whispered incoherently near my face. After I removed the business card he had tucked under my waistband, I pressed it into his groping fist and hissed, "Try someone else." And whatever his story was, whether sexually overdriven, hoping for yet another conquest, widowed, lonely, or terminally ill, I never slowed down long enough to care. I was so grown-up.

Living sensually should not have become a fucking liability, but it did. I was wholly reliant on, while undeniably accepting of, my expression of organic sensuality. After all, I had been thrown off course, led to deviate from normal since kindergarten. I habitually danced on dangerous boundaries cruelly disguised as trust and love. "Fuck off," I added as I walked away, ashamed and uncertain whether my response did damage or good.

Outside my children's bedroom that night in the bathroom, the eyelash glue was set; the phone rang. The agency apologized, the sitter had an emergency, another apology, but they had no staff left to replace her. "What? Wait, no. No! *Please?* There must be someone?" I was pleading.

"No, I'm sorry, dear," she said sweetly, firmly.

"Wait," I begged, "you don't understand, I can't just not show . . ."

"You won't be charged, dear, we're very . . ." her voice was trailing.

"No," fell from my lips, and I disintegrated, pathetic.

"Mama?" from their darkened room. "Mama?" again from my womb. But my limbs were limp. "Mama?" and I was falling, gripping the sink; I was sinking to the floor, falling backward, eyelashes glued together, eyelashes heavy and oozing, mixing with mascara. I was powdered, blushing, sparkling, and falling backward into the bathtub. "Mama???" The showgirl—body tight, rippling, toned curves, graceful like the wind, eyeliner pooling in the eyes, stinging. I unbecame, unraveled. "*Mama*?!" they cried, and they began to inhale my mania, my failure. "*Mama*?!!!" I curled into the despair of my undoing.

The yellow pages wouldn't help (*little footsteps tiptoed closer*), and I'd already exhausted my options, "the angels," I called them, those columns of rescuers: Sitter City, Nanny Net, pp. 21-24 (*their hands rested on the bathtub's ledge, their smooth pink fingernails held it and me*). I rocked and rocked until I hummed, until I could face them.

There in the crack
the pinhole
the roaches and cold porcelain.
I had no one.
*I told you so*, bled from my heart.
I had no one.

"Mama?"

"Why are you in the bathtub, Mommy?" There they were, their tiny fingers, their eyes swollen; there I was, raccoon-faced, hands up protectively. There they were.

"I have such great news," I managed, grabbing and holding onto the tub's edge, "I don't have to go," and they pulled and pulled me up, and saved me. "Want to order a pizza?" Their eyes watched my face normalize. "Watch a movie?"

"Yessssss!" they whooped in unison, and their perfect hands and ears and elbows burrowed into the waste of me. And we embraced. Pulling out from my hold, they turned, and with small wet cloths they returned and returned and returned, over and over and over again, "Here, Mama," together, bowing themselves to me. "Let's clean you up."

In the living room we snuggled; we watched Disney. They sipped on sippy cups and loved on their chocolate milks. They transformed into the animations on the TV before them, the story lines and happy endings they knew by heart. Babysitters disguised as little children was what they were, tag-teaming me, parenting me.

KETCHUP ON RICE:

1) Boil rice.
2) Add ketchup.

*What would love do now? This is a marvelous question,
because you will always know the answer. It is like magic.
It is a cleansing, like a soap. It washes away all doubt,
all fear. It bathes the mind with the wisdom of the soul.*

—Neale Donald Walsch

As hard as I tried to ensure safety and normalcy for my little ones, as galactic as my love for them stood, the whiff of chaos was always in the air. Would my odds in dodging hardship have been better had I stayed married to their father? Can a parent ever truly shape absolutes, craft the healthiest, the happiest children? We try over and over to lead with love and navigate trials and errors without fear, but . . .

> *The essence of being human is that a person is*
> *a person through other persons. I need you to become all*
> *you can become, for me to become what I can become.*
> —Bishop Desmond Tutu

So, if I love you, but you fear, what then? And if you love me, but I fear, what next?

I know I don't know most things.

I know I meditate on love, a lot.

My hope is when we meet and I place my love in the lead you will do the same. As you lean in toward me and offer your love forward first, can we meet there, love on love, *and leave fear behind?*

"Which books tonight, guys? You choose," I asked. I was tired. They were wide awake.

"*Dazzle the Dinosaur!*" my little man said, and "Maybe the ghost pirate one."

"*Baker Bill,*" my baby girl chirped. "And *A Little Old Man.*"

"Good," I whispered. I weighed a thousand pounds on my futon bed, a flapping tailing tuna fish; I nosed my way back into the ocean's hold. "Bring them all to me," I said, pat-patting at my hip. "Let's read them all."

One in a Viking helmet and the other in a Mickey Mouse beanie, they shimmied over— warmly scented in devotion— and bent into our sacred stories.

My babies just wanted to be seen by me. They didn't need to be told how excellent they were, not then, not when they were so small. *You want to be seen*, I thought to myself, stepping into their shoes, becoming them. *Look at me, Mama*, I remembered to myself, *I'm right here.* But back then, when I was their little, I had no mouth.

I hadn't fantasized about being a mother like some others did. Had my mother? Had her mother before her? But that first day home with both of them, before Paul and I had split, alone with our year-and-a-half-old boy and one-day-old baby girl, I was not afraid to *love* them even while my body shook with incompetence.

When my son rounded his second birthday, I bought a potty toilet. *He's two*, I thought to myself (was it Dr. Spock who told me?), and it was time to get him out of diapers. Like tying shoelaces or learning to button a shirt, I figured he and I would handle it together in one day's time. In the morning I helped him out of his pajamas and sodden diaper, encouraged him to go play in his birthday suit. *He'll just tell me when he needs to go,* I thought confidently.

In the dining room we'd set up our outdoor play gym, and they both loved it for climbing and sliding and hiding. My young boy was already showing signs of powerful thighs and supple feet, a natural athlete. I watched as he conquered the structure, scaling the wall of blue plastic and tunneling through one of its cutout shapes, armadillo boy, a roly-poly bug, his shoulder cape of penny-colored curls flashing in front of my eyes. Standing, he swung out onto the yellow slide, and with an "oooooof, oooooof" each time he stuck and stuck on its sticky surface, his bared skin skidded; he stop-started down the slope. Solving the problem, he stood back up, turned around and crab-walked his reddened backside back up again. "Mama," he proclaimed before letting it fly, his fountain of piss arcing onto the gym; the platform under his perfect feet turned into a puddle. I watched as he watched it pool under his heels.

The first day of potty-training shenanigans ended at bedtime without any progress. Frustrated, I called Angela, a friend who was a professional nanny and worked for families along Chicago's wealthy North Shore.

"Whahwt?!" her British-accented tone sang toward me from the telephone. "Oh, love, you started his potty training *when?*" Her amusement soothed me. "For fuck sake, you are too much," she snorted and quaked. "Did you think you would be done with it in a day, bub?" she cried laughing, and I joined her, finally, relieved I hadn't failed. "Oh, my dear! It might take you months or a year!" I could tell she tried not to laugh too much at my expense, but my ignorance was too much for her, so she laughed while loving me, and ultimately guided me through my next steps.

Raised in England, Angela became my tutor, my sounding board, my turn toward a voice of reason, and an uncompromising opinion giver, all things I desperately needed. She showered me in friendship and sarcasm. She taught me tools for child-rearing. She was pure gold piercing dark skin, her ears and nose, her wrists, accessorizing her stunning natural beauty and calm. She was my guardian angel. "Children need to learn to see, hear, and trust on their own, mate. Their lenses are focused toward their way, not yours. See through their eyes, but keep them safe."

"Yes," I agreed, "my job is to keep them safe." It took me a long time to understand that what I had experienced when I was younger was not normal. With Angela's guidance, I bowed to my children's fragility. I never had all the answers, and I struggled every day with my decisions regarding their care, but I protected them.

The first time I paid someone to carve into my flesh with a tattoo needle, I was sitting in a barber's chair in a basement apartment on the West Side of Chicago. A friend of Paul's, or a friend of a friend of his, a cool chick, sexy, in a T-shirt and long skirt, Doc Martens, and cigarette asked, "You didn't drink last night, did you?" and laughed while handing me a Miller Lite.

I wanted a Fiorucci cherub on my belly, a vintage-styled angel with wings gating her blushing cheeks, tight baby doll blond curls, and sky-blue wide eyes with a tiny cherry-red kisser. I'd seen the image on the price tag of a raincoat I'd bought years before; it was a green plastic sheer cling wrap kind of thing I nailed on the wall of my apartment but never wore. "Right here," I said, pointing left of my belly button. It tickled that first millisecond before it charred and burned for the next couple of hours.

Then for thirty more years I gathered many more ink spots onto my skin. And I realized I never spent much more than a moment deciding on what tattoo I wanted before I sat down for one. My mood on one day led me to an image. My tattoos were not symbolic projections of my ideology or visual messages of my essence; they were snapshots of one day, *a moment's notice. I turned to ink and needle after divorce, after my children left my nest, after episodes of my mother's deteriorating health, after her death. My body, my heart, my broken heart. The artwork gunning into my skin revealed my "self," a chronology—doodles, poetry, imperfect life. A fumbler, a faller, a saboteur. The buzzing commenced, the blood rose through the skin, pooled. It was a call to meditate, to transport back to the ocean water, always the same, back into the water where my ancestors darted, where the winds whipped above me, and my survival in the deep was my genetic code; I swam.*

    *Tattoo me.*

> *Without prayer, I am afraid . . . and with prayer,*
> *I will heal fearful thought.*
> —Debra Engle

(I realized I had been praying all along. To whom? It was a matter of semantics, call it God, Love, Connection, Light. Call it a higher vibration, energy, Source. In my self-made sanctuaries, in the invisible escape havens where my movement/voice lived was where I experienced an abundance of sustained love, advancing hope and awe, calm in the darkened depths of the water; tattoo me.)

When I was nine, I jaywalked behind a semi-truck that was stopped at a corner stop sign. A car had come from the opposite direction, on the other side of the semi, which I hadn't seen. There was no way the driver of that car could have anticipated me walking out from behind the truck, just as there was no way I could have seen him before I did. I was lucky that day; I didn't die. The car screeched and skidded, steel hit my leg, and I was thrown onto the pavement—my fault. A reddened, pinched face appeared at the window, leaned out, "What are ya doing?! *What* are ya doing?" and he pounded the steering wheel each time he screamed "doing!" I hadn't realized I'd peed myself until after he sped off, after his cussing faded. I uncrumpled and stood up, pulled the wet corduroys away from my thighs, and cried. I knew I'd be in trouble if I told. I knew they'd say it was my fault.

Slowly I walked the next hour home, off the main roads and into neighborhoods, into front yards and backyards, touching swing sets and stopping to swing. Chains high to the overhead bar, I grabbed and bucked and swooped up to horizontal for a float before tucking backward and lifting off the seat on the rebound. Gripping tighter as the chains relaxed, I stared down at the dirt and gravel below me, timed my jump. I walked past low wired garden fences and ducked under roof-high pines, slid between pale purple and blue lilacs, the dense hedges.

At least, I imagined doing all of that. In reality, I waited in front of Bridgeman's ice cream parlor for my mother to pick me up, our prearranged plan before I'd left for school that morning: "Walk to Bridgeman's, and I'll pick you up outside." Inside I rubbed paper towels over my pants in the bathroom, up and down the pale-yellow velvet cords, and cried. Outside I held my hands and a bag of candy in front of the wet stain, gripped my Starbursts, Jolly Rancher sticks, and Razzles: "First it's a candy, then it's a gum. Little round Razzles are so much fun." I would go home with candy.

Later I saw the baseball-sized bump below my knee, a nighttime-blue goose egg. And later still I fell asleep and dreamt I was dead, dreamt I saw my gravestone. It was a tall stone rectangle of plain cement that leaned off-kilter in the ground in a sleepy hollow cemetery, with old oaks and beech trees canopying the graveyard; wide tunnels of moonlight streamed down the black winding roads. Block letters were chiseled into my marker: *Here lies Tuni, 9. Damned before a decade*, and then the dream glitched, like the film cracked or broke, and it kept snapping back a few seconds and then repeating itself over and over—my epitaph, floating again and again across the screen. The size of the font became larger and larger and then shrank smaller and smaller, closing in on my eyes and then receding, a constant fluctuating echo with an overlying strobe effect: *Damned before a decade. Damned before a decade.*

The following morning, my palms were crossed over my chest where I lay in bed. It took me several moments to decide whether I was alive or dead, whether I had dreamt up my gravestone. I squeezed my hands together, interlaced my fingers, and pinched my knuckles white. I was praying. I wasn't praying to *God* because I hadn't extricated my mother yet from that role. But I felt I was praying to ancestors or praying to unborn souls or to the sun's soul and the stars, and without a doubt I prayed to the wind because I relied so much on her embrace, her kiss, her teasing ways with direction, and how she drew my focus outward and inward simultaneously. I prayed to yesterday and tomorrow, to a source I was convinced I was connected to even though I had no name for it.

"Where'd that bump come from?" my mother asked a week later.

"What bump?" I replied. She pointed down at my leg. I pressed my palms together on my heart, shrugged my shoulders, and said, "Oh . . . I don't know," and prayed. "Maybe I got hit with a trench ball, in gym," I said. And lied and prayed.

When I reached my tenth birthday, I felt I had made it. I was going to be okay. I'd made it to a decade, and proved that it had only been a dream, fooled it. I was going to get more time after all. But I kept up the praying anyway. I was building my own faith.

*in morning.*
*darkness sheds at the dawn of sun*
*in quiet*
*the quiet's direction.*
*or a dream*
*and I am the universe*
*breathing*
*my aching bones and aging muscles shy again*
*from death's door*
*but breath remains, I am the universe*
*falling into moving meditation.*
*My knees crackle.*
*My feet pop.*
*My hands cracker jack.*
*I hunt for connection.*
*I breathe deeply into you.*
*touch and desire lead me back to the beginning,*
*to breath, to breath, to*
*breath.*

*Several corners of my home shelve treasures I caretake. Three*
*stones lie on my bathroom countertop, for now. One is from a*
*coastal hike I shared with one of my sons near San Francisco.*

*One is jagged and flat. I picked it up in Portugal, one among thousands all the same on a dirt road in between parcels of farmland, picked up on a hot and dusty day that followed the hot and dusty day before that, my daughter and me on a pilgrimage. The third stone, I stole from a riverbed's edge near my home, where I watched a man sit skipping rocks while his dog hunted. "Look at this one," I say to no one and wrap my hand around it, its color changing after I lick it.*

*Sometimes, the morning's ritual is derailed; for example,*
*it's not quiet.*
*And then perceptions quickly alter, darken, and separate.*
*but breath*
*and beauty*
*and gratitude*
*return, eventually.*
*Usually.*

# dream three

*I look on as a friend is decapitated. I am fascinated by the head continuing to function—eyes rolling, eyebrows lifting and questioning, an ear cocking—all for several minutes after its radical departure from the rest of the body. My gaze stays at the neck's edge, bloody, ragged, and barbaric. In the dream, I am obsessed with death and worry over its inevitability while celebrating its possibilities. I am of both minds and cannot let go of my pursuit to understand the unknown, the doom, the intoxication. I dream. I am deciding whether light or darkness awaits.*

*And free-fall.*

I had two daughters and three sons. They have captured both organically feminine and boldly masculine qualities. They have leaned into justice and support of human rights, civil rights, gender diversity, and the myriad of ways to develop loving relationships. In opposition to brushing truths under the rug, they have tugged on the uncomfortable threads of confrontation under their feet. They have sought empathy and compassion toward the planet and toward themselves. They have been unafraid to say, "I love you," unafraid to be vulnerable. They were my master teachers.

For me, mothering produced a new language, a template that enabled a different, improved telling of history. They taught me that power.

If a woman has the balls enough to say she was taken by force,
believe her. Victims narrating their experiences, externalizing
what they have internalized are engaging in a sacred cleanse,
a painful purging of truth; listen. Deflecting trauma into art,
music, performance can be transformative and powerful, but
taking control of the narrative and stripping the story away
from the predator's hands allows the victim's voice to hold the
floor, challenges the normative and old-fashioned paradigms:

are you sure
don't walk alone
know your surroundings
avoid being out late at night
watch your drink
dress conservatively
carry mace
move on
did you fight
were you flirting
you wanted it

instead of . . .

are you okay
what do you remember
tell me
you must've been so scared
I can't imagine how you managed to get through
how dare they
you were violated
you were an object
dehumanized
let's go rip his dick off.

Victims will remember details, the thoughts and codes
embedded in their bodies messaging them even as they were
being overpowered. They will remember what they saw
behind their squeezed tight eyelids. They will remember
the taste of the acid rising into the backs of their throats, the
pain pressuring their skulls, the color of the wood framing
the door, the time travel, the day of the week, the color of the
sheet, the taste of their own tongues, the blood, dying . . .

I was a flat-bottomed, watermelon-breasted, eternally barefoot, blissed out, domesticated and accomplished baby-making
machine for years. Five children, *bada-bing bada-boom*, when
all was said and done. When my firstborn aged up to fourteen,
though, there he was again, Aladdin, and sadly, I died again;
I grieved again. Unexpectedly, I became Jasmine facing my
son. I slipped into my son's deep melancholy black eyes, his
long, lean body and fair skin, his auburn hair, his intellect, his
athleticism, his beating trustful heart, his innocence. He was
in middle school, he was a point guard, I made him bologna-
and-mayo sandwiches on Pepperidge Farm white bread and
cut them on the diagonal, tucked them next to fruit boxes in
his bag lunches. I bought him Fruit Gushers. I called school
when he was sick, signed his homework. He rode a school bus.

I couldn't help it, the mourning. I remembered the emptiness, how dark and detached and alone I was. And at some
point, I looked into my fourteen-year-old's deep black eyes,
and I told him how I was raped when I was his age. I told
my son my story.

We shook in each other's arms and wept. I didn't know
if telling him was the right thing to do. But I knew then I
would eventually tell his four siblings as well, each during

their fourteenth years. Did telling my daughters make them more fearful or more informed? Did my story anger my sons? Did it make them better men? They all wept alongside me, each one.

They buffered and cuddled my life's second act. Their love and loyalty were so obvious. And because of them, I grew into a stronger and more competent caregiver: the daily lists, the *hundreds* of miles in a day's drive, circling the village without ever crossing the county line, cat litter scooped, dog shit bagged, laundry folded, lunches tucked, dinners menu-ed, baths and stories at bedtime, love stitched and knotted over, under every purpose, on repeat—joy.

We coached
caught
closeted
chewed
cinched
curled
cropped and cupped.
We candied generously.

There were cherry and berry, lemon and mint, chocolate and caramelly sugary kisses in colorful foils, Skittles and Twizzlers in backpacks under report cards. Years and years and years and years of board games, water parks, zoos, and aquariums, Christmas Day movies, nighttime books, fevers, colds and booster shots and Band-Aids, sports injuries by the hundreds. It was a blur of fireworks and learning curves, which I was honored to climb and fascinate over, alongside them.

But the moment I drove away from my oldest son's college dorm, him with his nervous fake-as-fuck wave, me breathless, I glitched again. And each time one found the college destined to receive them, I struggled more. I was losing my confidants, my teachers. I turned inward.

I got certified as a hatha yoga instructor and studied its ancient practices of soul diving, spirituality hunting, the coolness and heat of bodies. I learned more anatomy and physiology and became even more astonished by the body's magnificence. I saw fascia everywhere, explored its winding shapes, its sticky spider man weblike role in everything and thought deeply on how all of the human systems interrelated and how they factored seamlessly into the universe's systems as well. I slowed down into meditations and body talking.

I began to bring my movement practice into my room, kept it dark and quiet, and explored how my breaths steered my turns and tensions. Alone, I twisted and lengthened, exhaled my shoulders away from my ears. Alone, I let go of the tension in my jaw, relaxed my tongue inside my mouth. It was a quiet and solo practice. I was reliant only on the floor beneath me; time was flexible.

*I married a man.*
*coochie pop.*
*I married thrice rolling the dice.*
*children followed; five, abiding guides*
*I relied high and low*
*on them,*
*my tides.*

*and prayed,*
*for one more day.*

"Get your hair out of your eyes," my mother blared, "go brush your hair," which I never did before or after her drilling. My hair was her kryptonite, something she couldn't touch or change. The messier it was, the more she hated it. And its bedheaded silhouette made her uncomfortable. My hair. I had also stopped showering—too cold—and the more days in between proper hygiene, the bedhead-ier my hair. Ponytails and French twists slid into mess; fine and twisted birds' nests flourished atop my head. I wrung out the sweaty strands from dance and moved on. Coaled eyes over layers of gloss and sticky lips, eyes and lips.

Lipstick, gloss, lippy, lip balm started back when I was eleven. First it was Revlon's coffee bean from Woolworth's downtown Minneapolis in the IDS building. Then, Wet and Wild's stock number 135; I could find it almost anywhere. There were splurges of tiny tubs of goo from department stores, pink and sticky, that made me want to lick and pull between my teeth; I applied it even at night, right before bed, and woke up pink and sticky.

"Mama," my youngest once shared, "I never realized other moms didn't wear lipstick every day until recently," and I laughed at my sixteen-year-old wonder. What did he see out there? How did it shape his idea of me, loving me as he did, unconditionally? I would never know the entirety of him, would I? Those were gifts, those interiorities surfacing, blessings of vulnerability and trust I hadn't learned at his age. "I love you," I said.

But something about me was always a little bit *off*. In dance class, I situated my tights over my leotard instead of under, folded the waist down to the level of my hips. If I'd kept them at my waist, I felt full, but lowering them to my hips, I was turned on, perpetually wet—for myself—and it looked odd. An elastic band stretched mid-torso across my ribs collected them, helped remind me to stop hyperextending, anchored my upper body; it was an odd accessory. My identity had been ripped apart by both my mother and my father from such a young age; my cosmetic choices became highly charged, desperate calls for control.

I hated being cold. In the summer, I balled up in knits and scarves and winter hats, wore rubber sweat shorts over everything (meant to loosen soft tissue), which steam-heated my muscles.

I stared at my body every day. I married the mirror.

"How many tattoos do you have?" he asked, lying facedown on the massage table. I had steady work at a businessman's club in downtown Chicago as a massage therapist.

"I don't know," I lied. "A couple."

"I could never date someone who had tattoos," he continued, talking out of both the left and right side of his mouth. "I have six sisters. They'd never let that fly." My hands kneaded one shoulder, one side of his neck; my fingers softly pinched the muscles and fascia. He was younger than most of my other clients, closer to my age.

"You can go ahead and turn over," I said, tenting the top sheet and blanket over him. He rolled over, and I sat down on the rolling stool at the head of the table. He was now faceup, adjusting; he was very handsome. "But you have a tattoo on your right ankle, yes? A leprechaun, isn't it?" I asked. My hands addressed the tension at the base of his skull. He began rambling about his work; he was a businessman, charming out sales pitches and flow charts.

"Well, yes, I do," he said, opening his eyes. "I have a leprechaun, and let me introduce myself. I'm John." I balanced his head in the palm of my right hand, turned it to the left and admired his dark Irish profile, his darkest black eyelashes, miniature wisps echoing the curls on his head. His shoulders, I imagined, were crafted by dips and push-ups, his arms tennis-trained, football hands, rugby legs.

When the massage was finished, after a final press onto his forehead that continued over his shoulders and along the side of his body, after touching his thighs, knees, ankles, and feet, I said, "Take your time getting off the table. I recommend drinking lots of water, and listen to your sisters. Also," I winked, "I don't date my clients." He took a job in Minneapolis.

Months later inside the Ten Cat, Dan lit my cigarette where he and I stood at the bar and where he explained he was John's best friend ya de dah, such a great guy, something about a flat tire and a rental car from the airport, followed by a cool segue toward the White Sox versus the Cubs (Cubs, naturally), rugby in college, and "Whadda youse drinkin?" in his Chicago South Side cute; he was filling in for John, who was apparently late and theoretically meeting me for a date. Firing up his smoke after mine, Dan and I leaned onto the mahogany bar, as I asked him, "Is your friend actually coming?" Smoke filled my eyes and stung. I felt duped and dumb, until Dan's smile interrupted my downward spiral, and behind me, swarthy handsome John walked in, hugged Dan, and threw an arm across my shoulders, waving three fingers toward the bartender. We slipped into easy conversations, several pints, and billiards. John was a shark. His friend was a mensch. I drove myself home.

My second date with John, another flight in for him, was downtown at an Irish bar in the Loop, Miller's Pub. Kelly-green awning, kelly-green booths, brass and dark wood with a deep Chicago history. John had beaten me there that time and was waiting outside under the awning in a black leather jacket, smiling. We sat in the window, side by side on stools, and I watched him closely, took note of his presence in public: a very single man, easily distracted by legs and heels clicking past him, tossing quickly his darting eyes toward other girls flipping their hair and fidgeting in their seats at the bar. He was impressed, impressive, impressionable. One beer in, I took the floor and gave him my history lesson: previously married, ex-dancer. I then pedaled slower and detailed my two little babies at home—names, ages, red hair, dark hair, dark eyes both of them, perfect saviors, blessings. He was unphased. We ordered two more. He was at home, I learned, bellied up to a bar, buying rounds, holding court, and becoming one with an old and ambienced, darkly lit pub. I was smitten—fell quickly for the young, handsome bachelor with the leprechaun tattoo, never-been-married, educated, employed, respectful. I thought, *Oh wow, oh wow.* And then, *Maybe I* won't *be a single mama for the rest of my life.* Because I was thirty-three and single with two young children, and I was on a second date with a man who appeared to enjoy my company, a decent, good man who remarkably didn't flinch at the thought of dating a family.

Years later, he joked he hadn't done his homework before jumping into our marriage with benefits. He had just kept opening car doors and restaurant doors and pub doors and picking up the tab and holding my hand. Our courtship continued between Minnesota and Chicago, with dinners for four, bedtime tuck-ins after Blockbuster rentals, cheering at youth soccer and T-ball games. He planted our butts in the third row behind home plate at Wrigley Field, a company perk I exploited as much as he allowed. A year later, the kids and I moved to Minnesota and rented the first floor of a duplex. It felt like a real home. We had a front door. We had a back door that led into a backyard. We made trips to my parents' house for frisbee and pickle, for swimming in the lake and tire swinging and cookouts. *He could charm a starving dog off a meat truck,* I thought, watching him read to my children.

He wore dress shoes without socks.

He had wicked hand-eye coordination.

He could sink a three-pointer nine times out of ten.

He drank gin and tonics with my mother, her legs triple-crossed over and under, her toes barely completing the final bend behind her ankle, her smile locked in. Was it the second or third time we had come for dinner, his entrance accompanied by "Hello, gorgeous" to my mother, a lullaby—was that all it took? I felt the same when he first said those words to me; it was a lovely feeling, but when he sang them to my mother and then again later when he met my Bubby, I felt just a little less gorgeous.

He drank red wine with my convivial father, wines my father collected from vineyards across the world. His cellar was a locked fortress containing thousands of merlots, cabernets, pinot noirs, chardonnays, rieslings. He warmly accepted my father's offer of a Cuban and puffed out the cocoa and leather, just like Dad.

Rounding our second year of dating, I actually gave him an ultimatum. I had two babies who looked forward to his good nights at bedtime and good mornings at dawn. On my knees, I begged the responsible, hardworking, driven, long-visional, compulsively organized, practical man who had effectively righted my ship, the man who inserted his love of politics, sports, wine, red meat and potatoes into our routine of Nickelodeon, sippy cups, naptimes, playtimes, mac and cheese and fish crackers, to call it.

He was a Wisconsin boy, one of ten children raised in a modest home a slingshot's distance away from thousands of acres of farmland. He was country roads. He was a small-town boy. We drove to his hometown with the kids one weekend, an easy day trip down Highway 94, and pulled into the driveway by midday. There were a couple of his siblings around; it was Labor Day weekend. Tall and open armed, his father gathered us in like a career PE teacher naturally would, a resonant welcome, echoing commentary. There was a long table in the kitchen that I tried imagining John and his siblings and parents, the twelve of them, sharing a meal around. I don't think it happened too many times given the twenty-or-so-year span between his oldest sister and his youngest brother, one in college, one in nursery school, final exams and state championships bridging naptimes and pep rallies, potlucks, and birthdays all year long; it had to have been chaotic. They were a faith-driven, athletic, intelligent family. During that visit we drove around Monroe, past the school he and his siblings attended, past their church, and the home of his first girlfriend, past the market where he worked in high school, past the sidewalks and the slowly murmuring elms and oaks on either side of them.

In the evening, he led me outside the home to sit with him under the night sky. That was not unusual for him, I already knew this, his awe of the constellations and galaxies and his love of a horizon that laid beyond farmland.

His sister came out right after us, sat next to me on the small bench on the front sidewalk and began to tell stories of John and his rescues, a bunny rabbit, an injured cat—"a habit of his," she said—nursing them back to health in cardboard boxes in their garage. "He was a caregiver," she wanted me to know. "I think we were a challenging group," she might have added, "and he was maybe lost there in the middle of all the craziness." I listened carefully, looked deeply into her eyes. I thought I understood her consoling smile and her faith in him.

I already knew he bent on one knee at night and prayed, elbows set on the mattress, hands folded together balancing his forehead, and I already understood there was a younger boy inside him, a humble boy who helped guide him into prayer.

On our way back home, again on Highway 94, John mumbled, "Let's pull off at this rest area," and suddenly his foot was braking and we pitched quickly down a ramp and around a corner into a small parking lot, a blanket of grass, a picnic table, a landmark plaque mounted on top of a large rock. He parked. "Wait here," he said over his shoulder, instructing the kids. He appeared to be angry, and I wasn't sure what or who might have done something to upset him. "We'll be right back," he ordered, walking away from the car. I shrugged at them in the back seat as they looked at each other and then back at me. I felt off-center, sensing a confrontation.

I watched his quick retreat up a small hill, his urgency. He wore a rust-colored flannel button-down and blended easily into the autumn palette, his black curls, jeans, his shirt, leaving us. I said to the kids, "Be right back," repeating what he had just said, before taking on the hill to join him.

I felt their heat coming in closer behind me, and then they were scrambling hand over leg onto the picnic table at the top of the hill. "Mama," they said, pointing to John, who was shivering, and then lowering himself to one knee. And there he was with closed eyes on one knee, biting his lip before lifting his hand and grabbing mine. And finally, there he was with his other hand, fumbling for too long in one pocket before trying a different pocket, pulling a small velvet jewelry box out, a box the color of a clear autumn sky and big enough for a ring.

Our sweet babysitter, a friend named Jen, said, "Absolutely, I'll stay over, for however long you wish!" And off we went to Europe before the wedding, a prenuptial honeymoon, where we quickly learned we traveled easily together. Amsterdam for a few days, Athens for a few days, a ferry to Samos. In Samos, we arrived late in the evening. The small room we had reserved was tidy and overlooked a busy street bordering a boardwalk and the sea. We slept within that salty clutch, the tall windows and the following morning's briny breezes, the billowing cotton curtains curling and waving off of rippling currents of air. We heard heels and hooves, military marching, a unified troop performing stiff legs, stiff boots, horses alongside, a parade's rhythm, a backbeat for our bodies, keeping up, the clicking, the droning all penetrating us through our widely opened windows.

The dampened sheets, the fading sound of soldiers marching, the sun raying golden light on the walls and bed, the cracked walls and sheer white curtains waltzing, lapping, a memory made itself solid as I knew it would.

We held hands climbing cobbled hills—or maybe some were brick—and hiked alongside pale stucco walls containing pale stucco homes, fuchsia blooms, and dark greens and powder blues reaching over barriers, curtaining livelihoods and sleep and children and families. We touched as we moved and came upon a hookah shop and joined the row of hunched-over bearded men, each one alone with his pipe, facing the road in worn laced boots and brown coats, hairy hands at the cuffs, puffs—the Aegean.

I wore baby doll dresses, a pixie, tight over my breasts, tender from love, Doc Marten combat boots flat-heeled and dirty. We ate Greek olives, feta and tomatoes, creamy hummus and oil, hunks spread onto warmed pita for breakfast. We watched each other swallow. He, in a black cotton shirt or a yellow cotton shirt, in jeans, in hiking boots. We ate gyros and salted fish and biscuits, drank buckets of black coffee. A small ferry sailed us to Turkey where we spun another bed in a tiny stone castle.

My mother had traveled long ago to the town of Assos with my father. She loved the stark beauty, the caramelly landscape meeting the walls of blue-gray water, the stones.

I wondered how the melancholy imprint of Assos fed their conversations, my mother's and father's. Were they altered somehow, was their connection deepened as they traveled along its dramatic shoreline, or did they experience it without caresses between them, companionable observers? Did she imagine herself there loved, turning over before the sun rose, touching him awake? Where did her love for him begin and end?

Assos was sculpted in dark brick and built into untamed hillsides, guarded by dry-stacked stone walls, and further inland, rolling grasses connected the low arcing bridges built over small riverbeds, more darkened rock spilling into the rivers and isolated lean-tos nearly falling into the overgrown landscapes. Old men, old spirits, old souls making memories with the sea. I paid attention, as if it was my last day, to the chipping weather, the flaking dried urchins, sea life clinging and falling from the wall I sat on, looking out because alone I saw not a trace of my fear, and following the blink of my eye I focused on only one step at a time, following the wind at my fingertips. "I would not waste time," I whispered to the old men fishing and shuffling, the seabirds' songs, mist, fog, wet, cool stones, "I would not take anything for granted."

"I love you," I said to John.

"I love you too," John said back, sitting next to me.

We drove to Istanbul and looked north over the endless Black Sea toward Odessa, a city of gypsies, where some of my ancestors had come from, the city for whom I named my daughter. We walked to the Hagia Sophia Mosque, and unable to go inside, we stepped into the Blue Mosque instead, received a small prayer rug and knelt; I slipped easily into mindfulness entering the space, let go of time, emptied my mind, and became my simplest form.

Always holding hands, we paved the days together, climbed into art galleries, slowed in the markets, sank into color and abundance, stood for fresh falafel and slow roasted lamb, grape leaves and honeyed baklava.

"Please," the proprietor insisted, "please sit." He of olive skin and gracious nod. And his son or brother, another young man who looked like him, brought us tea in small cups of hand-crafted glass, golden spoons, and a ceramic plate of fat dried dates. In ceremony, he performed, instructed us, "Like this," and he stepped and lowered his torso, his lips to the glass, and demonstrated a hot sip, a chewed edge of date, a lean back, and a tip up of his head. He nodded and smiled toward us, "Please." Finally, he unfolded the handwoven wools and knotted silks, the unpiling and folding and piling of hundreds of rugs.

John was handsome.
and neat
and honorable.
He was an achiever,
a tough go-getter.
Confident.
Very confident.
Armored.

In Turkey, I felt the lead in my thighs, a heaviness I sensed whether walking or at rest, and I began to ache through the very center of my pelvis, where a baby might catch and hold. It must have been in Athens, I had decided, where we saw the Parthenon from the low wide bed, and where the bed-sheets felt stiff and the window's dirty glass veiled the ancient craftmanship on top of the hill, over buried souls, the Persian rubble, Athena. Faded yellow draperies hung from broken rusted rods. I knew that leaden heaviness in my thighs; I knew I was pregnant.

"Please let me make it to the wedding day," I prayed. "Please let me carry the baby to term," eyes closed, praying. I prayed for every next minute.

My wedding dress was tailor-made, a bronzed mushroom silk, a bias cut that swept the floor, a tulip cherishing the dropped waist on up to my décolletage, a small train twirling from my behind. I felt elegant, wore my grandmother's diamond necklace, no veil, champagne-colored shoes that sparkled, peek-a-booed from under the gown. My low belly beat against my bouquet of blown-out roses, peonies, and camelias.

Our ceremony was held on the northside of town in a flower shop, in a warehouse in downtown Minneapolis in the middle of winter. It was blizzarding, sideways slanting, having its way with the bundled commuters outside. The city was buried. Streets became ice; the cars parked on them disappeared under mountains of wet, white peaks. Towering banks built from the plows lined the curbs, avalanching in reverse over the upper edges of the street signs.

Inside we were floral steamed heat. Inside we were Old and New Testament, stemware smashed underfoot, rings exchanged. Votives flickered when the drafts reached them; wet and icy water sweated and flowed under the window seams, flowed onto berried pine wreaths and mossed topiaries, baby's breath. A baby's breath, I still prayed.

The judge wore small round glasses and pronounced his lines formally from memory; his hands were unexpressive, professional, and dear—a judge in a flower shop, a Minnesota January, a snowstorm. Uncle Pennybags, I thought, from Monopoly, was who he reminded me of. ". . . given all these conditions, I believe marriage to be the best and most important relationship that can exist between two human beings . . ." I had read his draft previously, given it the thumbs-up. "There must be complete equality of both sides . . .no interference with mutual freedom . . . complete physical and mental intimacy." John was rescuing me, I was thinking. We both knew it. He was allowing me to slow my life down. We admired and respected each other. We got out of each other's way. The details of who decided what and when were left unspoken.

*Shoo be doo whop, shoo be doo wheep wheep, shoo be doo whop whop whop.* Jazz brought the heat to us as we arrived at the restaurant, brushing winter's wonderland from our shoulders. Jivey guitar backed up by a handsome beard-thrumming bass, a suited dude pop-dropping xylophone, and swinging dreads vocalizing smooth, ceiling-cracking smoky scat. Filet mignons and sea bass arrived on buttered potatoes. Family and friends happy-tapped into ske-dat delicacies and champagne toasts. Family and friends sweetened their tongues in lemon frosting, raspberry cake, and Dixieland. "Thank God," I swore I heard. "She did it."

Our daughter was born in July, a son was born two years later, and another son was born three years after that. We became altogether, seven.

I
nursed
swathed
bathed
polished
dipped
fluffed
folded
corrected
soothed

tickled
tucked
argued
disciplined
mended.
I hobbied.
I read.
I got a good night's sleep about eight years later.

*We do not want merely to see beauty, though,
God knows, even that is bounty enough. We want
something else which can hardly be put into words—to be
united with the beauty we see, to pass into it, to receive it
into ourselves, to bathe in it, to become part of it.*
—C. S. Lewis

# part three

## FAMILY

*Hands of beauty. The oldest ones that cannot uncrook them-selves but persist anyway to reach, hovering on futility. Ancient hands quivering, bones waterfalling under paper flesh, too much skin, dried tissue; an atrophied finger stubborn and weak and determined to touch, determined to open the door in front of her. "Take my hand, Mama, I will help you."*

*Baby hands, dimpled, fat, pudgy, yum. Fingers float and feel around space, anemones; fingers wrapping and octopus twisting, a reflex; a pinky's hook, a nose clutch, a nipple loved; toes. "I'm yours."*

*Hands of friendship, fingers interlaced, palm to palm, swinging and kicking up the heart's beat, pendulum love. "I love you."*

*Hands on heart, hers, captured and cold. The soul of her had left on angels' wings minutes or hours before I'd placed mine there. "Take me with you. What am I supposed to do now?"*

*hands up*
*handsome*
*hand over*
*handshake*
*handheld*

*handmaid*
*handmade.*
*hand off.*

*One of my mother's golden rules: "In the kitchen, make certain there is a window over your kitchen sink." Daydream, I thought.* Solid advice, to prioritize portals. *And I hustled the forks and knives and pimped dirty dishes while the rumbling bees bumbled outside and blue jays and thrumming rains filled my sink. And mustard weeds and the wind and emptiness.*

 *The idea of preparing to meditate puzzles me. Why? Why must permission to connect be scheduled? Must I sit on a cushion, with my legs crossed?*

*"We used to bathe together," my mother said to me suddenly during one of those times she was in the hospital. "Bub and I bathed together—I remember it." She had lowered her oxygen mask. "We sat in the bathtub, home from the beach, washing the sand off from between my legs." She looked at me slowly, rheumy, wrinkled, connected from every angle to the walls, to the machines. "Mommy," she said to me, confused, "I'm sorry I was naughty, Mommy." She got the fucking COVID.*

When I was small, I would sit in the bathroom with my mother, to be near her as she bathed. With one hand, her ritual, she lifted her breast, a soft sandbag, and kneaded and soaped underneath it, folded her washcloth around it, circled

the towel around and around. Her breasts. I sat and memorized them, her. I wanted to grow up and do that, be her. I
wanted to clean breasts like she did.

She lifted her legs one at a time, cupped them one
at a time with her palm. Delicate piles of bubbles fell from
the slope underneath her calf. She held time quietly, held her
razor and shaved over her ankle, her shin, her knee, her back
relaxed, uncurled a little, less twisted. She was beautiful.

*Eventually, reluctantly, standing at my kitchen sink, in
front of a kitchen window, I wondered what I would make
for dinner, and just as quickly, another breath, I lost my way
again through the glass into the bushes, a snake in the weeds.*

My mother's last apartment didn't have a window over
the kitchen sink. She no longer had the strength to stand
unassisted. She scowled when she saw me, like the day before
that one, all the same, until she realized I was watching her
scowl and was inwardly reminded of being better, of being
human, of beauty. She scowled because she was alone no
matter who was in the room with her. She hadn't opened a
window in years. She hadn't smelled soggy wood chips after
a rainstorm or smelly stinkhorns and their pungent aroma of
blood and musky death stalks. She hadn't smelled the roses.

# dream four

*I dreamt my mother and I wed. She insisted that the only way we could move forward through life was in matrimony, a union for better or worse, and we stood and took vows of forever. I was quiet and invisibly inconsolable, aware of the collaboration and the consequences, aware I was giving up.*

"Do you have any regrets?" she asked me.

"What do you mean?" I replied, and then continued, "Do you?" knowing exactly what I wanted her to say, praying she would let it go, praying, "I am sorry," would come from her lips.

"No," she said, and paused. "Only, I wish I would have left your father earlier."

Maybe that was it.

Her eyes leaked sorrow. Her eyes swam in the bunker of the lifetimes that lay between us. Her eyes fell from mine.

Her thumb and forefinger rubbed back and forth, agitated where they rested on her thigh, pilling the nothingness there, worrying the years of *I am sorry* between the soft and puckered dry pads of her fingertips, forming an invisible apology, so I believed. Her eyes returned finally to the room, her small bedroom. The blinds were drawn, keeping the sun's midday rays from lighting the aged folds of her skin, her lengthened nose and ears, her thickened gray combed hair.

"No, Mama." I sat down beside her and pulled her hands into both of mine. "I don't think I believe in regrets."

I inherited my mother's skin tone, her long legs and short-waisted torso. I inherited her scowl, her resting pissed-off face (I preferred to call it a fish mouth), an alluring pout. I inherited her love of fashion, but unlike my daughters who have alternately borrowed, stolen, pilfered, and swapped their clothing in and my clothing out of my closet, the only time I ever wore in public anything that belonged to my mother was the night I was married in a flower shop in a blizzard—married in the floor-length, wine velvet winter coat I huddled into after the ceremony.

I inherited (late) her love of literature. I guess I inherited her love of gay men, which is weird to write but accurate, if not socially incorrect or in bad taste to say, but the fact is, my mother gathered many, many male friends who happened to be homosexual, who happened to become more like sons to her than friends, whom she trusted and never felt threatened by. I get that.

I inherited her love of textiles and jewelry, and fine art and shoes. I inherited her slim calves and ankles, her tan lips. I inherited her tidiness, which seemed to translate into a brush-under-the-rug manifesto; if it looked nice, it was nice.

I inherited her love of animals, specifically dogs. And I inherited her admiration and mad respect for my father's genius piano skills and his expertise in hematology and oncology, his life-saving skills. He gave patients hope when they possibly had none and provided more time for those who thought they had none left. We both admired exceptionalisms.

I inherited my father's smooth fingertips and his silky hands. I inherited his quirkiness, awkwardness, clumsiness, some aspects of his creative and weird mind, his love of the exotic and exceptionally made.

*The creepy smoothness of my hands and my father's hands was misleading; they were smooth not because they contained moisture but because they were parched. They didn't scale, peel or flake or redden, which was also deceiving; they were slick. And when his skin touched my skin—his fingertips same as mine, his hands same as mine—they slipped.*

When I grew older, my father's smooth touch repulsed me. And a generation later, the slippery touch I inherited was noticed by my son who told me more than once, "Your fingertips are too smooth," and he flinched and pulled away from me and my maternal reach, his reaction innocently replicating the reaction I'd had to my father. "It's not you, Mama," said my son when he noticed my heart crack. "It's just too smooth; it's just your skin." I was grateful he told me. Then I agonized over my inheritance.

*His slippery touch that wasn't quite a tickle, nor was it firm, was a tease, a temptation, and it was brushed under the rug.*

(I inherited my grandmother's joie de vivre, a small shard of her soul.)

God was not something anyone talked about in my childhood home. And if in conversation the concept of God was inferred, it was immediately dismissed; God didn't exist. My grandmother practiced her Jewish faith, as did my cousins, but my immediate family practiced nothing. Once we moved into the suburbs and away from Bubby, her rituals, her support of the temple and Zionism, became a memory.

I longed for connection. And somehow, as only a child would do, I came up with the idea that my mother was The Actual God. Literally. It was how I explained to myself why we weren't taught about God. Because she was it. The idea both comforted and terrified me.

I understood, I believed my friends' mothers were only mothers, and their fathers were simply fathers. But somehow, I was convinced that my mother was human enough to birth me and my siblings but was also in charge of the universe—ominous, overly powerful, and perfect. "Are you God?" I asked her over and over. And she smiled and shrugged. "Are you God?" again and again.

"What do you think?" She tipped her head.

"Mama, are you God?"

"Maybe," she said.

I imagined her body floating with the stars, her body dissolving and reappearing and comet-ing around galaxies, plunging, nose-diving back to earth, back into our home, temporarily, because when I was asleep, she rocketed back up into space to take care of other more important things up in the heavens.

This carried on until the Tooth Fairy and Santa Claus and the Easter Bunny ceased to exist, which was also about the same time my father's touches stopped and when I stopped falling asleep on my mother in her bed, on her thrumping heartbeats, the maternal rhythms of the underworld.

I had wanted to ask my mother why he had done that, why dad had stopped touching me, but her pecking and cawing at me, as though I was her predator, kept me silent. God was mysterious.

# dream five

*My chin is tipped up, I am searching; it is cool along the shore. Some of my hair is stuck and poking into the four corners of my eyes and the sand is building and caking between my toes and I am scratched by the sharp, waterless weeds of the sea crunching under my feet, passing salt into the cracks of my soles, so I step more carefully. I am assured. Because I am alive. I fish and hook with finger and thumbs to pull the strands of hair from my eyes; the wind snaps and returns them to my wilder whipping mane.*

 *I fly inside the night sky moving away from the ocean's waves and thundering water. I am pounding and crashing my body upward through the earth's atmosphere. I am accelerating toward planets and stars as their shines layer promises into my light. I have finished competing with the squawking gulls, ospreys' calls. Their claws splay and tense because they envy my expansion. I am closer and closer to gas and flames, fireballs and meteoroids that distract me from the underworld I have left, the blackened landscape, the memories of my ancestors. It is Lord Ganesha I see replacing the moon, her rolling thighs and eyes wider than mine, her smiling belching laughter. Her massive form shifts alongside the constellations, blinking, winking, she applauds; she is emptying the sea.*

*She is fat and then lean, both. Her trunk lifts—she is a pun, an elephant joking herself into human form and then riddling herself back to Mastodon. She is pleased lifting mighty limbs, hurtling questions great distances toward the roiling oceans. She demands witnesses! "Commemorate her!" she commands to the earth below. And then to me she winks, "Press your wings; lasso the air. Join the fiery glory infinite, and move, move, move as we do. Watch me!" Lord Ganesha chants, "Come, miracle." She is pulsing, "Come to me."*

*I lift and pulse my feathers and ride the wind's tricky channels. I bank and tilt and turn. I am crop dusting and bumping into the air's tilting lanes until I have become one of everything. Planets and rings plunge through me, swarm me, burn and become me.*

*"Welcome," she purrs, and offers me her bed. "Sleep," she continues. "Those who survive the flight return to nothingness, the eternal light," and I nod and nestle into her calm; I turn into her heavy heaving breasts and part the Milking Ways. The air below me knits itself together, mending the path I had opened the moment before.*

*"Can you collect stones, triangular ones for the dead?" she whispers from nowhere. I do not see her, but I load my arms full until the burden of bearing is complete. Reappearing, Lord Ganesha and I arrange the risen, honor the dead.*

When I was younger, I was given a purple one-speed Schwinn, low barred for a girl. I rode in summertime circles around the block, roads to nowhere because I had strict boundaries and was instructed to stay close to home. Many years later, I bought a yellow Specialized, a twenty-one-speed hybrid. A *Stump-jumper*. Meant for city roads, dirt roads, and off-road tracks, I rode it to and from work every day. No longer dancing, I was selling outdoor gear. I rode hard and fast, helmeted, head-phones on, the Sony Walkman tucked into my waistband. I swerved recklessly around buses and cabs, ran reds, flipped off haters. On weekends, I skidded around with friends entering mud races and obstacle courses, raced triathlons, duathlons, and dirt courses; it substituted for the thrill of dance in many ways: the training, the diet, the costuming, the performance, crossing the finish line. It exhausted my body, a habit I couldn't break. After my family and I moved to Ohio, I discovered Cleveland's Emerald Necklace, a gorgeous, jeweled chain of parks circling Cleveland with walking paths, wooded hikes, waterfalls, rivers, rapids, swimming, biking, campgrounds and playgrounds—a community treasure. I took advantage of the rolling hills, dips and dives, miles and miles of standing climbs and bomb-dropping descents, miles of riverside rides.

But the wintertime stalled my momentum a bit, and I eventually swapped the iced-over roads for an indoor sweatbox cycling studio. With a handful of other obsessive cyclists, side by side, we spun, belched, farted, queefed, and snotted. Clipped in, we rode nowhere with the Foo Fighters, Third Eye Blind, Mumford and Sons, and Prince. It was cult sweat.

I spotted a ballet barre in the corner outside the cycling room one day and asked the studio owner, a friend, if she'd allow me to use it. "Yes, mama!" she said. "Let me know when—I'll get you a key. You can let yourself in and lock up when done."

It was like hooking up with an old lover, easy as air, nourishing, stirring. I wore jeans that first time as a way of backing in, as a way of lowering my expectations. I wasn't doing this for real, I reasoned; I was touching base, reconnecting with an old flame. But immediately, the heart of the matter rose up. My jeans fused with the energy in my legs, and I was electrified. Like a first blistering kiss.

I began spending less time biking and more time back at the barre. One thing led to another, and I accepted a teaching position at a nearby performing arts center. Unlike my experiences teaching decades before, this time I was ready to embrace a leadership role. Unlike before when I pushed my students into a rigid template of "do it my way," I eased up. I softened into my students' learning abilities and watched them more carefully, and instead of demanding right and wrong from them, I tried to develop my teaching style by stepping into their shoes. I allowed them to guide me, minute by minute, to where our classes needed to go, where our focus needed to be.

The art center was small, and classes labeled "advanced" included kids with a wide variety of skills; the center preferred to have a class populated by students of the same age rather than of the same level of skill. By allowing my students' needs to show me the way, we all benefitted from insights we may not have otherwise been exposed to. When I taught a beginner the appropriate placement of her chin in a forward tendu, I would catch the more advanced students checking themselves, experimenting with épaulement. When I asked the more advanced students to initiate their movements from deep within their belly or their pelvic floor or from their heart centers, I witnessed the beginners nodding appreciatively as though leaning into a rare secret. It was challenging to keep the various levels engaged and progressing all at once, but I believed we succeeded. I thought it was extraordinary.

The director of the art center asked me to resurrect her pre-professional youth dance company, so I reconnected with former colleagues and friends from Chicago and New York, and by spring the company was touring and performing. I hired master teachers for weekend-long workshops and pulled in students from outside our school's roster. Word of mouth escalated, and women with talented daughters wanted in. I began to look at my dance knowledge and experience in a new way, as unique and valuable. And I watched as my choreography, embodied by my students, gave truth to a voice I had for so long kept quiet. My rhythms, my shapes, my visions, my fantasy world presented through their bodies were astounding.

"Why don't you open your own studio?" my friends asked me. The idea terrified and wowed me. I had never imagined doing such a thing. But I knew it made sense—that unless I was in charge, I would invariably be making creative concessions for someone else. I knew I had the work ethic and drive to give it a shot. What I didn't have was any knowledge of how to run a business, nor was I certain I could put together a following large enough to sustain my own studio. I risked losing money; I risked becoming a public failure. But the encouragement from friends continued, and my studio, T Move, was born.

I had developed my own hybrid of a barre class. I used CrossFit bands and therapy bands to assist clients, help them sense their bodies as I wanted them to. In the 1950s, dancer Lotte Berk came up with the idea of connecting dance technique to a fitness platform and had immediate success. So I followed her lead and ran adult barre classes in the mornings and dance classes in the evenings.

As I became aware of the vulnerabilities I experienced running my own dance studio, I was reminded of when I first became a single mother. How incredibly hard that was, how I felt constantly judged. What made sense to me at that time, and what my childhood dissociations had initiated in me before then, was that if I didn't take care of myself and prioritize my well-being, I couldn't be the best possible version of myself for anyone—not for my children and not for me. I knew that opening the studio was speaking to that because once I committed to the ginormosity of owning and directing my own studio, a sweet sacredness returned to my way of being; I knew deep down I was again taking care of myself—a soul connection, and I could relax into my uncertainties, dismiss second-guessing myself.

I leased a 1,000-square-foot space in an upscale village mall minutes from our home in the suburb of Cleveland where I lived. Construction was minimal: drywalled partitions came down, carpeting was pulled up, and mirrors were hot-glued onto the walls. Old-school oak wood ballet barres were bolted in.

An old metal shelving rack became storage for my exercise equipment: resistance bands, dumbbells, stability disks, fitness balls. A reclaimed tool bench was topped with galvanized steel and became my check-in counter where I manned the ship, the schedule, the payments, the music. Every detail was achingly important to me; I was manifesting my identity in a small box with mirrors. I wanted love first, community second, and magic third—there was no way the wisdom of dance and movement would be left behind; I knew that was an impossibility. An odd wooden chicken feeder I found held hair ties, business cards, and stickers with love quotes. I held firm on my selection of light fixtures (three supersized whimsical dandelion globes that never belonged in a ballet studio; the dancers literally swerved around them or their tour jetés would have knocked them down, but the flowered fluff added wishes and dreams into the room). I fell in love with and bought a mounted standing buffalo skull. He was a two-feet-tall, three-dimensional Georgia O'Keeffe nod and sigh. It stood at the front door where it improbably became the studio mascot, spawning underwear adorned with its image for sale, tolerating lights during the holidays and seasonal dress-ups. I installed a 55-inch flat-screen TV and imagined all kinds of uses for it, like filming the dancers and watching playback on the big screen so they could evaluate themselves in real time or downloading clips of famous per-formers, educational videos, and movies for slumber parties.

It was opening day. Clients readied themselves at the barre for our first class, "murder barre," as some called it. I liked being known as a task master. I worked alongside my clients with the effort my teenage self had honed all those years ago and brought an elite athlete's mindset to an adult workout class. In actuality, the exercises barely differed from most other barre classes. Ultimately, the camaraderie and loyalty of my clientele made the classes hard; as a community they kept themselves and each other accountable by always showing up. The TV was on, and images of my dancers, our build-out, friends, and family cycled across its screen. I was streaming *feelings*, what the studio meant to me, what I'd hoped it would come to mean for my clientele.

Ritually, habitually, in the very last moment before I would teach, I'd go pee. Even if I didn't think I had to go, it was part of my pregame warm-up. "We will start in one minute," I called out, and rushed to the restroom down the hall where I pissed like a racehorse, like a raging fire hose of a let go. And fuck if I didn't forget to pull my knickers down with my leggings. And for fuck's sake I couldn't do anything but watch it fly, watch it drench and saturate and soak my underwear, until I was roaring hysterically on the can, relief and humility trading places with my nerves and ego.

I was becoming a public role model and felt humbled by that responsibility. With that leap, I had to come out of my own body shame, and I knew I needed to reflect what I preached, to walk my talk—most especially for my young dancers—and show strength and beauty without shame.

"I want them removed," I said at that first visit.

"I won't be able to do that for you unless you replace them with new ones," the cosmetic surgeon explained, "smaller if you wish, but after all this time, you won't be happy with any result unless you reimplant."

And so, back to my laptop to search for the right surgeon, a surgeon who would take them out and leave them out. I told my clients why I would be gone for two weeks, and many thought I'd gone mad.

"You have the perfect figure," one said, "I would die to have those."

"You're crazy," from another.

The doctor photographed me, topless, up against the wall of her office. I stood in front of her projector that cast lines, intersected and divided my breasts, coursed down through my nipples, and split them in halves and quarters—a preemptive faux slicing and dicing, a refashioning of my tits that would result in the removal of all of the silicone and leave me close to my original form. I inhaled deeply, reflexively pulled my stomach in, pulled my vulnerability in.

"I can do it," she pronounced. "I can't promise you will completely love the result. This isn't how I'd normally perform this procedure."

"It's fine," I cut her off. "It's what I want."

I woke up in my own bed, propped high on a mountain of pillows. I was mummy-wrapped in dressing tape from my lower rib cage up to my collarbone, corseted in white tape. It was hard to breathe.

I woke up in my own bed, hot, terrified, constricted. I pulled my chin in, peered down my nose, crossed my eyes to try and glimpse my chest, which was gone.

"Are you awake, Mama?" One of my kids was bedside. I woke up in my bed, crying quietly, tears smoothly rolling from the outsides of my eyes to my jaw and under my jaw-line, into my ears. I was awake.

"Yes, honey, I am awake." I smiled.

"I love you, Mama," one whispered, all of my children whispered, over and over.

On either side of my rib cage, there were three-inch plastic vials filling with bright red blood. I would empty them as needed and pour the blood down the sink until by the end of the second week post-op, the vials remained only as a safety net. I was healing well enough to go back to work; it was time to move. By the end of that second week, I was back teaching. Intentionally, I chose workout clothing that was comfortable but at the same time didn't hide the significant change in my silhouette: leggings, knee-high socks, a body-hugging leotard, a head scarf. The bandages and vials that caught the discharging fluids were held in place by the leotard. No one asked me about the surgery. No one commented on the change in my appearance. For my clients, my first day back after a two-week absence was just another day at the studio. For me, it was a symbolic return to self-love. I had lopped off decades of shame, confronted fear head-on, stood my ground. I was flat and true.

My kids were damned proud of me. And the studio took off. Classes were full and I needed more staff. We offered ballet, pointe, modern, lyrical, hip-hop, tap, acro, silks, yoga, Broadway dance, flash mobs, charity gigs, school shows, parades, and festivals. I had five-year-olds learning beside high schoolers learning beside octogenarians. I choreographed a hip-hop routine for seniors who lived nearby in an assisted living home, and they went on to perform it as an opening act in a film festival. My pre-professional youth company performed several times in New York, filmed a music video in downtown Cleveland, and performed with the Cleveland Opera. All under the name of T Move, a dream.

*It's not the weight you carry but how you carry it—*
*books, bricks, grief—*
*it's all in the way*
*you embrace it, balance it, carry it*
—MARY OLIVER

My father died three years later. My niece died a month
after that. My heart cracked open. My husband got a job
in Indianapolis. I closed the studio. My heart cracked open
again. We moved to Indy.

# dream six, please

*My eyes are closed, I am underwater, I am racing fast along the river's current, I am riding the inhales and exhales—the rushing dark passageways of flow. I am gaming eternity. I touch between my legs and rub and rub and quickly cum, and then swim off, mind and body ravished. Tuni-fish.*

The day before it happened, we'd made our first field trip into downtown Indianapolis. I bought tickets for a catacomb tour, a dusty grotto. Above the catacomb on street level once stood a grand performance hall. We followed the tour guide down several staircases and long hallways to a heavy door. Beyond that we single-filed a boardwalk path that zigzagged over the dirt below it. Some of the coves on either side of the boardwalk were lit by hanging light bulbs, and our guide's torches pointed toward them saying ghosts cornered themselves there.

"How much did we pay to walk around an old basement?" my husband sassed, which drew an echo and a smirk from my son.

"It was fun," I said afterward, squinting into the daylight. It was a Saturday, and we had no plans except to wander around our brand-new hometown, discover its character, learn its history.

A wedding party in fuchsia, black, and white posed for a photographer on the stone steps of the Soldiers' and Sailors' Monument. We walked toward them. My hair was tucked behind my ears. I wore orange framed sunglasses. I had pink lippy on, Lululemon leggings, and flip-flops. My T-shirt was green with a mermaid printed across my chest. My son photo-clicked and captured John and me up and sideways away from the newly wedded couple, sitting in the sun. It was hot that day, and when we eventually arrived back home, we wished our new home's pool had been serviced. It would have been so nice to cool off and wash the underground dust off, but we hadn't scheduled that maintenance yet. We had only moved to Indiana the week before, and we didn't realize it would be so hot in early June, in Indianapolis, so hot that we would want a swim.

"No . . ." I tried that word. I tried to say it.

And then, I heard her whisper, "Don't move," near me, near my right ear. Was she crouching, or was she very small? I thought she smelled sweet like caramel, like a chocolate star (my friend Angela in Chicago was likely who I was thinking of). I pictured her in a long white dress and an apron wild with colors, tied around her. "Help is coming," she hummed, and "Please don't move, sweetie."

I was praising her, worshipping her. I was curled into a small ball. "Where is your face?" I wanted to see her face. But I couldn't move or speak. I couldn't open my eyes. "Help is coming, *fa la la*," like a gospel.

It was Father's Day. One of my daughters had come home to visit, to surprise her daddy, the day before. She was the one who helped him load my bike into his car after the EMTs arrived. She was the one who drove his car down and found us after he phoned her. (I guess she would have seen me motionless, curled into a strange and angled fetal position on that bike path, or maybe she saw me tensing and gritting, popping in and out of reality, out of existence like quantum foam, like foamy 7UP.)

I was sticks and branches, limbs split open, torn and protruding where they weren't meant to be; I was a weather event. I remembered they tried moving me, and I think I muffly screamed. I was an aftermath, an explosion, so they waited until the morphine slid all the way in before rolling me onto a gurney. I remembered the siren, once or twice. I remembered the hospital like downtown traffic—commutive, a hallway of beds, stopping and starting, side cars of IV fluid stands shifting in and out of lanes. During one of my checkups two years after the accident, I asked the doctor to fill in the timeline for me. I felt so fortunate that she'd been the one on call that day, that she'd put me back together. I wanted to know how it went down, what happened when she first met me. She told me she'd asked me a bunch of questions like, "Can you move your thumb up and down? Can you show me four fingers up?" and "How about turning your palm to the ceiling?" and "Make a fist?" Of course I didn't remember any of that. It was a blindside that took me months to piece together: my bike spun out, a week in the hospital, and then a year of Frankenstein arms.

"I looked at your X-rays," she continued, "and we had a chat." But what about the woman who kneeled next to my ear and sang to me, the one who told me to lie still, the one whose soft whispers cradled and rocked me until blackout? I wanted to know her because she had guardian angel-ed me too.

I had worn a black Stella McCartney swimsuit and a black bike skort for that Father's Day ride. Rescue professionals scissored up the middle of me to cut them off. I remembered that.

John and I had both checked my brakes and the air in my tires. I had clipped in and out of my pedals a couple of times, which I always did before riding. I liked to feel the ease of the clip in and to feel the release as I swiveled my shoe out.

What I later learned was that my bike had been disassembled and assembled improperly by the company who had moved us to Indiana. It was a bike that was not to be taken apart but transported, just rolled on to a moving truck. I'd even had it serviced right before we moved. They'd lost a piece, or forgotten it, but a part needed for the shaft that connected the body of the bike to the handlebar was missing.

My left wrist had broken in two and required a steel plate and some screws. My right elbow had shattered into several pieces, including one that poked a hole through my skin. I would eventually become bionic.

My recovery included two years of rehabilitation, three surgeries, one bone stimulator, half a year of brain-emptying narcotics, and neuropathy pain that nearly ended me.

We hadn't finished emptying the boxes yet. We hadn't hung pictures on the walls yet. In Indianapolis, I was friendless. During the first couple weeks, my older kids took turns coming home to help me.

Percocet, Valium, hydrocodone, OxyContin—every fourth hour, by the minute. I set my alarm and never missed a dose. My breath, my sweat, my snot, and my tears reeked of burnt plastic and acetone. I lingered days on end, nowhere. My eyes stayed wide open. Rooms relentlessly spun. I struggled getting out of bed, but I wouldn't miss that dose. I pressed my body in millimeters, wormed like a moving stone, like make believe, back and forth, like a journey out of deep earth. Arching my back so that my body weight dropped to my shoulder blades, I inchwormed myself with my feet first, then my shoulder girdle toward the headboard of the bed. I could then brace myself there, use the resistance of the headboard to swivel my lower body off the bed and slide upright into a seated position, like a tragic cartoon. I was terrified. Once vertical, it was only the world I feared. I had no mind. I had no movement. I had fear.

To feel safe, I shuffled as I pressed myself against the edge of my bed. As I pushed my weight against the mattress and as I stepped, I was afraid of one foot following the next. I knew if I wandered, if I tipped away from the safety of the bed, if I walked out into open space, I would fall. After ten minutes,

I arrived at my bathroom sink twenty feet away. Tiny Indian brass bowls along the counter were filled with pain relief. Those altar bowls had been given to me by a friend years before. They were meant to be filled with sacred objects that could symbolize a connection toward the spiritual world.

All I had to do was bend my knees, tip my weaving body over carefully, and tongue the pills into my mouth. The fingertips of my left hand peeked out of its splint just enough to push the faucet handle forward. Since I was already tipped, I turned my face sideways and sucked in a drop of water, then curled my fingertips behind the faucet handle to shut off the water. I slid my body back along the wall, reversed my steps until I was back to my side of the bed, and slowly lowered myself onto the mattress. Into an exhale, I lay back down. If I also had to pee, it added up to an hour of exercise.

"My arm is on fire!" I was screaming. "NO!" I screamed. "NO!" I screamed. I imploded. *My arm is burning alive.* From my fingertips to my armpit, I caught fire. An hour earlier, desperate to get off the drugs, I had skipped one dose. And then my arm caught fire.

Angela, my rock. Angela had serendipitously phoned me just at that moment. My phone had serendipitously been sitting on the bed right next to me where I had curled myself into a ball, where I was writhing and thrashing, where I was knotting myself into the bedding. The phone rang, her name flashing. I curled my left fingers around it, pulled it close, and with one finger pressed go and screamed. She didn't skip a beat. "Get back on them now," she demanded. "You get someone in there and you get back on them and you don't stop taking them until your doctor says so. You'll get through this." I knew she had said that to me because she always said things like that to me: "You'll get through this." "You will be okay. Who's home? Who's with you? You have to be smart."

"Angela," was all I managed. I remember she stayed with me on the phone until the panic and fear backed down. "Please help me." I tried to get a body in the room.

Angela called someone, one of my kids. Someone who had flown home for me. Someone rushed in with my drugs. "You're going to be okay," she kept saying; she kept phoning me over and over until her fear had subsided too. She saved me.

*The self,*
*the identity I formed as a very young girl was in large part informed by arousal. The child mind learned and interpreted in the dark while snuggled into sheets and a matching comforter that said sleep, sleep.*
*I*
*was aroused.*

*On red city buses, I traveled from school into the city. I stared into homes through windows at the beautiful and sensual possibilities that lay within them. I peered down the side streets and at playgrounds, bridges, skyways, people. I wanted to know what joined everything together. Did everything pivot on arousal like I did, to survive?*
*Until*
*I was older, and in order to remain safe, I became quiet and afraid, and I lashed out and exploded and self-destructed enough to suck all the air out of the day. I stopped seeing what lay beyond me, suppressed wonder.*
*But, in time,*
*I learned,*
*all of us,*
*all of us,*
*all of us*

are keeping score, on our knees, on a scorecard. Trauma wisdom in our cells, in our bloodstreams, and in our precious hearts.

But what if the child mind had been given a do-it-yourself manual, a heartsmith handbook containing what the traveled mind knows to be true. What if, right from the start, we had all been given an atlas for love that plainly outlined on the map the pain and sorrow of being human, but also had clear directions for guiding us toward the sacred roads and paths of heart connections, like a TripTik with rest stops and starred destinations offering rewards for kindness to those who visited and vending machine prizes for random acts of kindness, and for paying attention.

And what if at the bottom of those maps, inside that handy atlas, in very small print, there were footnotes mentioning the roads leading nowhere, the hiding places, alarming detours, trauma's quicksand, and the ego's domain; a warning to be cautious.


*Attention is the rarest and purest form of generosity.*
—Simone Weil

I was child mind again but fifty years older. I was wonder and awe. My physical improvements were painfully slow, but my mind was drawn further into healing and further out to giving. In gratitude, I sought joy. In gratitude, I became a hospice volunteer.

I plugged an address into my phone's map app. Two years in Indianapolis spent recovering, I was still unfamiliar with my landscape and relied heavily on Siri.

On that day, I drove about an hour to meet Anne W. I could be easily distracted while driving through new surroundings or by Bon Iver or Iron & Wine or Ben Howard or John Butler or Kanye or Graham Nash or RY X or Active Child or Pearl Jam or Nine Inch Nails.

The building looked a little off, I thought as I parked and glanced at it; it was underwhelming. I gathered my things, organized my thoughts, and got out of my car. I'd been to many senior homes at this point, no two the same.

I pressed the buzzer alongside the door, and through it I saw a check-in area on the left, a window, a desk behind the window, taped cartoons on the window, holiday decorations. The door swung open, surprising me, and an older, smartly dressed woman appeared and said, "Are you coming in?" She wasn't glamorous like a Ginger. She was more like my Bubby's housekeeper, Mrs. Walta, competent, pleasantly curved, and well-ordered.

She nodded and smiled as I stepped toward her and said, "Thank you so much." I noticed her beige cardigan, the short fur collar, her matching flared slacks, the knotted silk floral scarf at her neck. "Would you happen to know . . . I am looking for . . ." opening the folder I had brought with me, "Anne in room . . ." fumbling.

"Yes, yes, of course I know Anne, dear Anne," she said. "She is up those stairs right there and down the hall on the right-hand side," and she pointed up the narrow staircase as she drew me through the door and past the empty office. "She'll be so happy to see you," she said, adjusting her sweater, revealing a more weathered figure than I'd first noticed, large heavy breasts, folds at her bra strap, her waistline, dimples. A *cuddler*, I thought.

"Oh, great. Thanks again," I replied, and watched her step through the front door and leave before I turned.

The carpeting on the stairs was dirty and worn in the middle, another beige, threadbare in places. There was a heavy smell of frying oil, old as though it had been built into

the foundation or painted onto the walls. As I arrived on the
top stair, I saw two older women whispering together in the
hallway, each in front of their own doorway it seemed, but
the hallway was so narrow their bodies couldn't avoid meeting and touching. I saw their tenderness; one hand stayed on
the other's waist as their bodies leaned toward each other
until their foreheads met in the middle. They were rhythmic,
like a pulse.

I was always a little nervous meeting a patient for the
first time. Some didn't want visitors. My entrance needed to
be positive and loving and would hopefully bend potential
apprehensions into ease. Sometimes, all I did was trade places
with the air in the room, quiet and still next to quiet and still.

"Sorry, excuse me," I said, stepping closer to them.
"Would you happen to know, is Anne . . ."

"You'll probably have to knock more than once," they
said in unison. "Loudly!" and they laughed.

"Perfect, thank you!" I said, trying to join them, trying
to hitch a ride on their lovely vibe. On my left I passed a
room with beauty salon chairs in it, three in a row, old-fashioned chairs with molded plastic dryers as big as beach balls
fastened to the backs of them. I remembered going with my
mother to her hair appointments when I was little, and she'd
sit with her hair foiled in strips under a dryer just like that,
or sometimes in curlers, and she'd smoke or read a magazine
or a newspaper, and I'd always wanted to do that, sit under
one of those huge plastic helmets. I loved the beauty salon,
and she'd give me a penny for the gumball machine up front,
and once I put the penny in, I prayed for it to spill out too
many Chiclets, like an accidental bonus, which sometimes
happened. My teeth cut through the gum's crunch, and the
flecks of crispy sugar coated the inside of my mouth.

I tapped on Anne's door, waited, tapped again, and
looked back toward the women, but they'd gone. I knocked

louder and finally heard a shuffling, a nothing, a shuffling. The door opened slightly, and an uncertain eye appeared.

"Hi, Anne," I said, slowly, "I'm Tuni, I'm a volunteer from Anew . . ." but the door closed.

Opening it again, wider the second time, half-smiling, she asked, "Want to come in?"

She was shorter than I. She was soft armed and soft chinned, and her thinned hair was teased and lacquered into a back-combed beehive. I didn't at first notice the tobacco smell, but her voice and skin broadcast a habit. I learned later that she also chewed. She scooped up a well-behaved pup, a toy something, a miniature blend. I introduced myself again and asked if it was okay for me to visit a bit. "May I sit down?" I smiled.

Seated, I could prepare myself better for tender or melancholy or sacred or tragic. I slowed down the visuals of her room, watched her body language, and allowed faith and love to guide me.

"Yes, sit." She pointed to the couch, and I followed her. "Here," she said, and I sat down beside her. She leaned a little into the sofa's arm at her back, leaned away from me.

First, I asked about her health; her paperwork mentioned heart issues. And we spoke about her living space, which was nice! She had a New York City–sized studio kitchen, a kitchen counter the width of a window, a mini fridge, a quart-sized steel sink. She had a four-top electric range and a kettle for hot water. A very functional room was what I had thought.

Christmas was near, and her room was decorated. In the corner stood an artificial tree strung with colored lights, silver garland, and Hallmark ornaments, most of them identical. A rumpled red tree skirt lay underneath with dog toys on it. On the window ledge stood a row of small, pipe-smoking Santa Clauses next to reindeer and elves. Peppermint candies filled a small glass dish, and some of the wrappers lay on the floor below it.

"What's your dog's name?" I asked. And, tickling the pup, she introduced her as "Phoebe." The dog's dander lifted swiftly as Anne's strokes became firmer. Remnants of cigarette smoke and sweet perfume floated through the room.

Anne began to relax and open up to me. Her deadbeat husband had left her fifteen years ago. Her son, her angel, died of an overdose just before her husband left. Her daughter married a drug dealer, but Anne hadn't spoken to her in a decade—not until recently when she had decided to call and apologize for disowning her. But she didn't understand how her daughter could have married a drug dealer; hadn't they had enough trouble? But her daughter wouldn't listen, and her attempt at reconciliation was dismissed.

Anne told me she got around alright but that her hips troubled her. "The staircase is hard for me to climb down," she admitted in her gravelly voice. "I use my cane, but it's hard for me to remember which goes first, the cane or the foot. Then I miss a step, and I think I'm going to fall. It scares me. I don't like stairs." I wondered if Anne should be on oxygen because her respiration was becoming more labored with every minute.

"You're pretty," she said, catching me off guard, and I thanked her.

"You're pretty too," I replied, and she showed me that face, the eyes that draw up into the top eyelids and the nose and chin that dive down in disbelief.

But she smiled. "I have a hard time breathing," she continued, and so I took a chance and asked, "Then why do you smoke?" But that embarrassed her, and I immediately regretted asking. She said she only smoked when she could get herself outside the building, "But I hate those stairs, so when it's really cold or icy outside, I just open my window and blow the smoke out that way."

But that confused me, and I pressed one more time, "But I'm surprised the staff allows you to smoke?" I couldn't imagine how she was getting away with smoking in her room. But she changed the subject, circled back again to her "dead beat" ex-husband, who had just recently died.

She continued, "And I'm glad he's dead 'cause he started comin' by around me uninvited, begging me for money and bein' rude." She paused, and as though she had just registered the last thing I had said to her, she asked, "Who is going to stop me from smoking?" And with her head tilting back and her eyes popping, she began to laugh hysterically. "Who the hell is going to stop me?"

It was about at that moment when I thought back to the kind woman who had opened the door for me when I had first arrived, with her fashion-forward ensemble, the tasteful silk scarf, and polite manner. I thought about how she generously guided me toward Anne's room, beyond the empty office with Post-it Notes on its window and the small sign in the corner that read: *Closed Tuesdays, Thursdays, Saturdays, and Sundays.* And I remembered right before I took those stairs up and smelled the heavy cooking oil in the walls of the building, I'd thought, *Well, that's odd. Why would the front reception office be around only a few days of the week?* but I remembered I'd been noticing the worn carpeting on the staircase and then the two affectionate women at the top of the stairs.

And while Anne's hysterical laughter began escalating into snorts and fits of coughing, I remembered how enchanting the hair dryers were and how they had reminded me of my mother in curlers or foils, and the Chiclets. That was when I realized I hadn't actually seen a single nurse, doctor, aide, or piece of medical equipment—I hadn't seen anything resembling a medical device, anywhere.

Grabbing my folder, I opened it and showed her the name written on the top page. "Who is Anne Walls?" she asked, her nose and eyes scrunching, her face a twisted joyful butterfly knot.

"Oh . . . my . . . *God*," I said under my breath, crossing my legs. And we howled and hawed and dissolved into pure nonsense.

"My name is Anne Washington!" she rejoiced after I managed to explain my mistake through the laughter. Anne Washington, my dear new friend who lived in an apartment building next to a big parking lot behind an Arby's drive-through, across from a Walgreen's. Anne Washington, who wasn't imminently dying or being treated for a terminal illness. Anne Washington, who was a widow estranged from her daughter and who lived close to an assisted living home in northwest Indiana. Anne Washington, who lost her only son to an overdose. Anne Washington was lonely.

"Will you come back and see me again next week?!" she sang and pleaded through the laughter. "PLEASE come back and see me!" she screamed, waving me down the hall of her apartment building.

I found the senior home where I was meant to be, and where Anne *Walls* lived, a three minutes' drive from Anne Washington's apartment. I entered the facility with the very proper signage over the canopied circular drive and checked in with the receptionist, then proceeded to walk past a few nurses gathered at their stations. I found Anne Walls. Her mouth was slightly open, and her lower jaw fell a little off to the left, a little unhinged. The television was on, muted, bolted up near the ceiling in her dark room. Her face was TV blue. She was sound asleep.

It was a mystery I never solved, how I'd ended up in Anne Washington's apartment, an accidental, magnificent, heart-correcting moment along my way.

I saw hearts cracking open all around me. And I wanted to help, however small my impact might be. I felt honored when I stepped into a hospice environment.

His was at the end of a long, sour hallway; his door was closed. I walked up to it for the first time in late August. I knocked softly first, and since there was no response, I knocked again, louder, and attempted an introduction from behind it. Finally, I pushed the door a tiny bit open and with a stronger voice said, "Hello, John. My name is Tuni, and I'm a hospice volunteer. May I come in?"

"Yes, Yes! Come in! Why didn't you knock?" he snapped. I pulled on the lanyard, showing my credentials, growing taller. I heard the agitation in his response, pessimism, annoyance.

The smell inside the room was putrid. I sipped inhales as I stepped in, blew my exhales out, kept my hand over my mouth. Beyond the bathroom on my left, beyond the wall after the bathroom, and past that corner, I saw him in bed. "Hi John," I introduced myself again.

His face scrambled. His eyes popped and jockeyed out of their sockets and spun. He was gaunt and yellow, with tight skin barely covering his skull. I imagined struts holding his bones in place, sliding sideways and outward from the center of his body. Half of his face wandered sharply away from the other half; every part of him simultaneously shifted. I outstretched my hand closer to him; was I hallucinating? He suddenly self-corrected, like a science fiction Transformer robot, a jerking-off reassemblage of his arms, his shoulder girdle, his face, his rib cage, his spine, his eyes. My eyes were tricking me. He emerged back together again and softened. He was in recognizable human form; he coyishly smiled and said, "Well, hello . . ."

Below his waistline, underneath the gray wool blanket, were his limbs, like an afterthought. I could see them, the two thin rows created by them, but they looked decorative, like a stiff, a whiff, like an awkward mannequin. His button-down flannel shirt hung from his collarbones, and when he spoke, the shirt puffed out like a pufferfish, blowing up and out as he spoke.

"If it's alright with you, may I sit a while? We could have a little chat?" I located a chair. It was behind a medical cart and a storage cabinet, buried in the corner in front of the window. I was sweating. There was a field on the other side of that window, woods, birds, sky, and air.

He was suddenly agitated about his appearance. He wet his fingertips and pulled thin strands of his dark hair toward the side and back of his skull, away from his sallow, pallid face. He unbuttoned his collar.

"Tell me your name again!" he hollered. "Nurse! Nurse! Come in here! Meet the visitor!" And a nurse did come in, stayed close to the door and smiled.

"Is everything alright in here, John?"

"Hi," I said, "I'm Tuni," and stood up briefly from the chair. "Nice to meet you."

"What a blessing this is! What a day!" he raved. "In my room, well, well!"

And the nurse turned around, "Well then, good," she said, "if there's nothing else," and her words floated in the air behind her, like kisses.

*Hemorrhoid* was embroidered above the breast pocket of his shirt. "Do you think that's funny?" he was plunging himself into me, prodding me in order to release some kind of reaction, I thought. And as though I wouldn't have already read it, he mocked me, "Read what it says on my shirt! Read that word right there," and he pounded his chest, again and again, "HEM-orrrrhooiid!" like a ringmaster, and again, "Hemorrrrhooiid!" to the crowds.

All of his shirts were the same; four of them hung in his closet, with the same embroidery over the breast pocket. He told me he'd paid someone to do the stitching for him. "Those laundry ladies think I'm hilarious; they love it!" he said. "Those fat farts won't mess up my shirts no more! They know those shirts belong to me!"

"Yes," I lied, "that's pretty funny."

The room air was overwhelming, the stench of him. "Do you think it would be alright if I opened the window?" I asked. "Maybe get some fresh air in here?"

"Yes, yes! Absolutely, open it up, a marvelous idea!" he said with great dramatic flourish, like he stood with a seal, with a dancing lion.

I had that feeling again of wanting to slow down time, to try and peer further back into John's story and find the ways in which we were more alike than different, find our connection. I needed to do that before I succumbed to his performance, before he ate me up.

It was a late summer day that felt more like an autumn day, there was a brisk, crisp breeze that blew into the room, and after I opened the window the breeze thinned the piss-and-funky-shit atmosphere. I sat back down and faced him in his bed. I prayed we could soften together. I prayed he would settle himself down. He scared me to death.

I never met his family members, so I never had the benefit of a relative's account of him. He told me he had two sons and a wife. He was sixty-seven in hospice, in a facility that also housed his wife in a separate wing from him. His wife was also sixty-seven, but she required memory care because of a terrible fall that resulted in her suffering significant brain damage. By the time the EMTs had arrived at their home after her fall, she had lost her pulse, and her breathing had stopped. John's two adult sons frantically begged the emergency staff to revive and save her. And they did.

John told me he had been disappointed his wife survived. (According to John, he loved his wife, but he was tired of taking care of her. He said her health had been deteriorating for a long time even before her fall.) He told me the amount of time she had spent in between life and death, when her brain had been deprived of oxygen, resulted in permanent brain damage. She never again had memory of her family. She wasn't able to walk, feed, clothe, or relieve herself without assistance, and the care required to manage her—which originally fell on to John—made him bitter. But he resented his sons. He told me he blamed them for worsening his life. Their needs, their pleas to the emergency medical staff to save their mama's life, had ruined his, he said.

A couple of years after his wife's accident, John had his. In his garage, he was trying to lift and move a high-voltage transformer when he fell off a low step while backing up. He became wedged in between the front of his pickup truck and the corner of the garage. It became impossible for him to hold the transformer. He fell under its weight and his leg was crushed. In the corner of his garage, his sickly wife inside, he passed out. It was hours before one of his sons stumbled upon him and called an ambulance.

After a week in the hospital, John checked himself out. His left leg had a fourth-degree burn, but somehow his bones remained intact. He was a retired long-haul trucker with little income and a lot of debt. He had no idea how he would be able to afford more medical care. He had no idea how he would manage caring for his wife.

But his leg was dying, and in time, an infection took hold of it. His sons soon after became overwhelmed with caring for both of them and admitted them into hospice care.

Glenda, the director of volunteers, had explained to me at the beginning that John was flagged as a challenging patient.

But the sons had pleaded with her to try one more volunteer. "Be mindful," she said. "If you ever feel uncomfortable while you're with him, we will reassign you, no questions asked." I told her it would be fine.

It wasn't until nearly two hours into my first visit that I witnessed a radical shift in his demeanor. It was when he began to talk about cars, long hauling, and automobile mechanics. I told him I drove a Jeep, a manual—said how much I enjoyed it.

He asked, "Would you know how to fix it? If it broke? Could you fix it?"

I replied, "Of course not." He became more animated, pitched forward on his bed. I told him I would bring my Jeep owner's manual the following week when I returned. He was smiling, looking human. "Would you be willing to explain a few things to me?" I soft-tossed. He asked what day I would be coming. He asked if I would come more than once a week. "No," I tried to dismiss my discomfort, "I probably won't be able to come more than once a week." I left exhausted and weepy and hopeful.

The following week, the air in John's room was less dense and his coloring was better. He had just been given a sponge bath by the nurse and was wearing a muscle shirt, a "wifebeater."

"Can you go get one of my shirts out of the closet?" he asked. I handed him a Hemorrhoid and barely missed the swinging urine bag hanging on the side of his bed. He buttoned up and patted down a few times along the front of his shirt, pleased to see me.

There was one photo on the ledge next to his bed, opposite me and the window. A family photo of four standing with shoulders touching, arms at their sides; a glossy picture in an 8-x-10 frame. In the photograph, John was much younger. He had a full head of hair and a wide smile. He wore polyester flared pants and a heavy brown button-down shirt, open at the collar, and he stood with his body turned slightly toward his wife. His wife wore a sweater that matched his shirt and a short skirt a shade darker, pantyhose, and small-heeled loafers. Her hair was teased and curled, and she had dimples. Their boys stood on either end, both of them in collared shirts, collars open at the neck, only the top button undone. Their lower jaws made them look like each other, locking their lips closed in a hurried smirk.

John was a trucker. He had lived in Quincy, an old mining town an hour southwest of Indianapolis, population 1,500, give or take. Three decades driving the Chicago circuit delivered him independence, a sense of authority, and little accountability. Sometimes he drove south to Tennessee and occasionally he'd gig to Texas. He did not like driving into Chicago, never appreciated the drivers "up there." They were rude and reckless. "They're asshole Yankees," he cocksured.

He taught me the difference between an eighteen-wheeler and a twenty-two. He bragged about chatting up fellow truckers along his routes and crudely gloated about roadway seductions and pissing off the cops. He loved auto mechanics and had several magazines devoted to the topic in the cabinet next to his bed, which eventually he pulled out to show me, one by one. But his legs never moved. He was a torso propped on a pelvis, and at any moment I was afraid he was going to shift and slide and discombobulate himself again, like he had the day we met.

He talked about depression. He confessed he had tried to kill himself, that he had been admitted to the VA hospital and put on suicide watch. I guess I felt I could handle his sadness, his defeats; I had wanted to support him. And once I'd leave, once he'd talked himself dry or I'd talked myself dry, I sat and cried in my car, in the parking lot. I didn't have the words or the medicine or the magic to save him, and I felt my best intentions—just sharing space with him and listening to him and responding to him—would never be enough to actually help him.

I brought him homemade cookies and cakes. I brought him miniature candies to add to his collection next to his bed—Heath bars, Snickers. He enjoyed hearing about my marriage, my kids, my dogs, and he especially loved my affection for Halloween. I told him how I created horrific Halloween dioramas outside my house every year. I explained how I transformed myself into the most wicked witch, ghoulish clown, deranged zombie. I confessed I thrilled a little when scaring children and scaring their fathers.

"Do you have photos?" he asked excitedly.

"Of course, I do," I said, and shared two decades of Halloween mayhem with him. "The fathers are the ones who get really scared; they don't trust me, I can tell. And I'll soothe the little ones if I need to. I'll show them my sweet side." John loved this.

The last time I saw him he was more agitated, impatient. He wondered if he had cancer, he told me, and he thought that if he did, he would take me with him.

I didn't understand what he meant and asked him to repeat it. "What do you mean, you would take me with you?"

His forehead was glistening, his lips were parched, his energy was spastic. He said, "If a doctor were to walk into the room right now and tell me I was going to die of cancer, I would grab you and take you to the grave with me. Yeah . . ." he laughed, "because I'm ready to go. I'm ready, and my ol' lady's gonna rot on that side," pointing to memory care, "while my leg's gonna keep on doin' nothin', right here. Give me cancer," he ranted, "but I'm takin' you with me!" and he began to howl.

I was stunned. His demeanor was shattering . . . splintering apart. "Have your sons come to see you yet today? Are they coming?" I stuttered; I was slipping, spinning. "I'm afraid I have to get going, John, I'm sorry," I rushed. "I'll be back same time next week, okay?" and I vanished.

"Hemorrhoid!" he hollered as I was walking out the door. "Did I scare you, Miss Tuni? Don't pass me up. I'm your old Hemorrhoid, honey." My heart cracked. I felt I failed him.

I knew I was required to report the incident and phoned my volunteer coordinator who contacted his social worker. The social worker called me. I was not to return to John's location until further notice. The next day she called me again to inform me his medical team was adjusting his medications. She admitted there had been previous issues similar to what I'd experienced reported in his file and advised me not to feel responsible for his behavior. I tried not to feel responsible or helpless or guilty. He was suffering, but I was able to walk away from him. The next day I picked up a voicemail from my volunteer coordinator. John had passed.

*Grief and gratitude are kindred souls, each pointing to the beauty of what is transient and given to us by grace.*
—PATRICIA CAMPBELL CARLSON

Ancestor.
Predecessor.
Beforehand.
Bubela.

She hummed or whistled as she walked around the lake located across the boulevard from her home, every day. Bub lived in that home for seventy-five years. It had a sprawling side yard where she placed two iron standing hammocks and a storage rack for her canoe. There was a long flower bed with reds, yellows, whites, and greens bordering the side yard, and lilies of the valley nearer to the house, low and enchanting near one of the elms.

The home had emerald awnings on every side—over the patio by the front door, over the back door and the porch, over the side windows. Across Lake of the Isles Parkway to the right was a historic stone bridge that crossed the lake's canal. And just beyond that, on the other side of the bridge, sat her fountain, a "bubbler" dedicated to her, memorializing her daily walks around the lake for many of her one hundred and one years.

I parked the rental car along the boulevard in front of her home. Sludge and muck saturated the floor underneath my boots; ice bundles stuck to my mittens and slowly melted and streamed toward my elbows underneath my shirt. My toes were Minnesota frozen, along with my nose, fingertips, ear tips, and chin. It was February.

But my thighs had a hint of warmth; they were grief leaden. And I struggled with the embedded dread in my legs while I clung to the possibility of mistaken news, a mix-up in the retelling or I'd misheard, misunderstood, and Bubby was napping, resting, awaiting my arrival. My legs buckled as though navigating a hard, cold sea, a winter current, the heaviness of an ocean storm making each of my steps forward to the shore futile, impossible, and doomed. First, one leg sank to the bottom of the snowbank, and I was down on my knees again.

From the car to the curb to the sidewalk I trudged toward her. I heaved my heart up the long stone steps and the hill to her house. A lifetime ago, I'd memorized its gracefully bent landscaping, an up and sideways slant to her front door. As a child, I'd made up a game—a simple gay dance onto each step. I'd counted my footsteps for each stair and paired it with a rhythm, a skip, a jump, a swivel, a glide, a swoosh, a hop, a slide. And I won the day from start to finish, as long as I didn't miss a step, avoided the cracks, and danced my entrance to Bubby, my prize.

I hugged my arms over my down jacket. I marked my time with a slow beat up those front yard steps. I stared at the doorbell.

When I was young, I'd played in every room of her home. There wasn't a door, cupboard, closet, or drawer unavailable to me. The glass jars of treats and bowls of nuts, the cases of sodas, the delicate glassware for basement games of "house" or "restaurant," my crowded meetings of make believe. I had free rein. And the most cherished place of all, her treasure-filled attic, was where I set sail on far-away adventures, found quiet, silence, and safety.

I'd slept on every bed in Bubby's house. I'd even slept on Mrs. Walta's bed after she died. I'd slept on the veranda, the back porch, the basement sofa, the pony room (named for the stuffed pony that lived there), and the chaise lounge next to Bubby's bed.

"Hi," I said to my mom when she opened the front door. Her eyes were dry and tired. She stayed behind the door as she opened it and backed up with baby steps.

Bub had died the day before. She had been in a coma, my mother told me, barely breathing, not waking up. I had pleaded with my mom on the phone when she had called, to keep her there. "Please, please," I had begged, "I'll get on the very next flight. I'll book right now." I needed to see her before she was packaged up, moved along. "Please."

Bub gave my mom permission to redecorate her own bedroom when she turned thirteen. "It was a standoff," my mom said, but Bub relented. My mom repainted the walls sky blue and picked out heavy floral valances for the windows, and matching sheets and comforter for her bed. Two of her windows overlooked the parkway, and the canal was almost visible from there. On hot, muggy summer nights, she told me she crossed over that street and slept on the bank of the canal overnight, a blanket under the stars.

Bubby's mother, "Daisy," lived with them during that time. She was the original occupant of the bedroom at the top of the back stairwell, the grayish-blue, creaking, narrow staircase that led to the third floor, the attic, the bathroom with its standing tub across from the bedroom large enough for the twin bed and its dresser—long before Mrs. Walta slept there. Grandma Daisy doted on her granddaughter, my mother, and she was the reason my mother chose to be called by that same name. Grandma Daisy cooked the stews and ruby-red borschts, the salmon molds and cottage cheese with everything: cheese blintzes, tuna balls, pies, apple cakes, and kugels.

She taught Bub embroidery. They made nursery-themed menageries with their silken threads. Bub stitched an alphabet, a bicycle, and a small pretty girl in a dress and fancy shoes along with my name and my birthday on one piece of fabric. It was framed and hung in my bedroom.

I loved the swimming oceans in the blue veins of Bub's hands that lifted in waves while she held the wooden embroidery hoop. I followed the stretching thin skin layered over her knuckles. I had just started noticing my own hands not long before Bub died, how they were just like hers and like my mother's, veined with waterways; I was wading behind them, bridging their arthritic knuckles to mine, their long noses, their olive skins, their lined and feathery lips.

Bub was on her back in bed, her hands resting over the bed linens on her chest, while her body was tucked in underneath the sheets. Her mouth was closed. She looked peaceful.

I watched and waited for her to flinch or scrunch or inhale or jerk or peek or turn her head toward me and smile. The ocean flowed behind her, wavy hair quieted her pillow, wavy hair sailed a peaceful winter's sea.

Often when I'd slept over when I was little, I would sit on her bed behind her and watch as she faced her dresser's mirror and brushed the length of her hair in long strokes. She unpinned her bun, hairpin after hairpin, narrow black metal arcs that nonsensically held her heavy hair up. She was always halfway undressed in her ivory-colored underwire bra and half-slip, her full waist and hips and breasts and shoulders plain and beautiful. But half-clothed, she kept her shoes on. She had bunions; her toe joints jutted into angry right angles as her feet squeezed into her narrow practical shoes, right up until the moment she went to sleep. But her back was straight and regal. She had a queen's spine, a proper and royal posture.

We had traveled to Israel together. She had offered to bring one of her grandchildren with her on a Hadassah trip, inviting each grandchild, starting with the eldest, until the open invitation eventually closed on me, the youngest of her eight grandchildren.

We slept the first few nights in Jerusalem, admired the ancient cityscape from our hotel room. "Tooner Pooner," Bub lullabied me. Her notes climbed the glass window we stood behind, our eyes and noses pressed into the view toward the ancient and modern limestone landscape, a monochrome skyline over centuries of war, bloodshed, devotion, and sacrifice.

Later, I glided my hand along the stonework laid for Kings of the Holy Land. We joined others praying, devout men davening up close and next to the Western Wall. I tentatively held the words I had written on a tiny piece of paper, a misfit's wish; dreamy, I folded and placed it in between two stones, sidestepping the Orthodox.

We were bussed to Masada and its fortresses, ghosts coming up through and from the underworld, their pale winds and shadows. The Israel Defense Forces, women and men, were stationed at bus stops, street corners, parks, and plazas. With M16 automatic assault rifles cross-strapping their bodies, they soldiered themselves everywhere along the State's parched earth, their mission: peace. We visited the dead in the National Military Cemetery. We visited Yad Vashem, where I stood gutted: photographs, books, journals, newspapers, teeth, prison wear, eyeglasses, strands of hair—a horrific Holocaust altar.

One of the final destinations on our trip was the Dead Sea. We were invited to receive massage treatments and finish with a float in the salty seawater. An older, balding man dressed in a white tunic gestured for me to follow him, turned down the sheet on the table, and pointed to where I could store my robe and slippers—a hook on the wall, a tray on the floor. I kept my eyes closed when he knocked and came back into the room. He lowered the lights. I fell asleep.

I woke because I had felt pressure, heat palming my vulva—his therapeutic hand—and then his fingers pinching and twisting my clit. And I came, while he hummed a quiet melody from the back of his throat. He finished, smiled, bowed, and left the room.

I had wanted to tell Bub, but I couldn't. I was ashamed. I found her outside in the sea afterward, already afloat, licking the ancient salt rocks from her lips under a cloudless blue sky.

*Did it happen to you as well?* I had wondered, and I'd actually prayed it had happened to her too. I didn't want to be the only one who would allow that to happen. But there she was like a far-off dream, eyes closed, luminous, like a loving light, my grandmother floating, waiting for me to join her on the dense Dead Sea.

The window was open in Bubby's bedroom. I'd felt the cool air coming in as I'd folded and then kneeled beside her. I placed my hand on both of hers. Frozen. Eventually, I moved to the easy chair on the other side of her bed near the window and sat to read the siddur I had brought with me, my small blue one. I chanted; I repeated the Mourner's Kaddish. I read through psalms.

*When I chant Hebrew, I lie down with the trope; I embody it. The tones and rhythms of the Torah, the psalms profoundly connect me to Source, to Light—a calling.*

A day later, I chanted at her gravesite God's cadence again. My rabbi had recorded its trope, and I'd memorized its haunting, sacred tones. El Malei Rachamim, the prayer that asks for merciful shelter under God's wings and peaceful repose in eternal life.

The summer before my father died, my family and I were with him, sharing our annual vacation time in the cottage he and my mother had purchased in the '70s. Our heartbeat cottage: Martha's Vineyard. My soul station: Martha's Vineyard. He hobbled then—barefoot—to the bathroom for his shower, a dramatic seesaw gait, pitch and wave, just like the buoy outside our kitchen window recovering from the passing boat in the channel. Again and again, *bong-bong,* his lopsided legs teetered and hitched, which was a result of his driving a rental car too fast on a winding road in the fog, skidding and slamming into a telephone pole. But that accident had happened years before then.

That summer, in the bathroom when he shaved, he swirled his neck, chin, and cheeks with a horsehair brush, frothing foamy *sandalwood oil soap all over. He used a metal razor to pull through the lather slowly from cheekbone to jawbone, outer face to inner, upper lip on the left and right, then from the base of his neck up to his chin. He finished with his sideburns, edging and squaring. He smelled of lavender, jasmine, rose, and earth for the rest of the day; the sweet wood scents migrated to his shirt collars and behind his neck, across his shoulders. He wore only boxers when he shaved, leaving the bathroom door open for the show, having just finished his shower. He wiped steam from the mirror just enough for his face to reflect back to him, leaned over the sink for the best look. He was very patient when he shaved, a mindful groomer.

"Your father has had an accident," my mother had phoned me ten years before then, "but he's going to make it." The accident that maimed him, hobbled his gait. Without his custom platform shoe made for his left foot, the right leg was six inches longer. He had stayed later that year, past that Labor Day weekend, and fog had complicated his flying home. But my mother had waited three full days to tell anyone about his accident. And I filled with fury once I'd received the news from her like an afterthought, the decades-long habit she had cultivated—manipulating details of him to suit her needs, to spite him. She had waited three days to tell us, removing the possibility of us investing our hopes in his survival. She was punishing him for being alive, for being a man, for ignoring her needs enough that she only had venom left in her tongue when she spoke to him or about him. Maybe she was punishing him in order to make up for her inability to intervene on my behalf all those years before. Maybe that was her way of apologizing to me, by despising him. It didn't matter. She was consistently angry toward him, so there really didn't need to be a reason why. I never heard him speak about his accident or whether or not he remembered any of it: being airlifted to the mainland, recovering and discovering he'd lost those six inches from his left femur bone. Had he been afraid? Was he surprised he survived? I never heard him say he cared either way.

My father witnessed a lot of death in his profession. He was a well-known oncologist and hematologist, he was sought after, he was the terminally diagnosed, dying man's expert, a final hope. Friends or acquaintances of my parents would phone my mother in desperation, hoping she would help connect them to him. My mother did take pride in his medical skills. And after he died, families and friends and relatives of his patients attended his memorial service and came forward to my mother in gratitude, hundreds and hundreds of people thankful for the extension of time my father had given their loved ones. That was meaningful to my mother.

He was a faithful breakfast man. And when vacationing alongside my father that summer, I knew when morning had begun, because he had entered the kitchen. The timing of his breakfast never wavered, just as the fishermen were finding the sea and the night of fog was lifting and the gulls began to sing. He had shaven, he had dressed, and he was preparing to tuck into breakfast, clockwork.

The kitchen drawers and cupboards were opened and shut loudly; the toaster oven door would squeak before springing shut. His breakfast prep orchestra was clamorous; it was eight a.m.

Each day, my father mizzled half of a grapefruit with honey (the second half of that grapefruit he would eat the following day); yellow skinned and pink fleshed, the fruit bled its juices at his mouth, which he dabbed properly with a white paper napkin. He slid his toasted slice of sourdough under a soured pungent soft cheese and then schmeared Tiptree orange marmalade into the dairy, speckling it with slivers of bitter citrus peel. He drank his coffee black. And with both elbows on the table around his plate, between his ravenously large bites, he read the *New York Times*. Tiptree marmalade was produced in small batches, in copper pans, on a farm in England, a detail that was important to him, a hint at the eccentricities of his personality.

My father played piano as a mad scientist might: inspired, angry, obsessively. He stumbled through his mistakes, stopped to pencil in notes, and then resumed his musical mania. His skin breathed out Rachmaninoff and Mahler; his bones banged Schubert and Beethoven. Those complicated rhythms and patterns he crafted and perfected became, of course, my anatomy, my nervous system, my skin and bones.

He meticulously researched all of his passions: pens, watches, socks, bow ties, cuff links, authors, playwrights, composers. He loved stereos, boats, and automobiles, Great Danes and gardening; everything he touched and handled, inhaled, sampled, swallowed, sat on, slept in, was tragically flawless. His laugh was bladder-splitting, terrifying and infectious. His appetite, gluttonous.

My mother, I think, was in love with the idea of him— his passions, his classical intellect, his sophisticated palate. After all, she was, at one point, the target of all three of those things. But in his grand expansiveness, his desire for the magnificent and extraordinary, his relentless pursuit of perfection, he sort of missed, often dismissed the smaller moments in their lives together. He bungled intimacy and overlooked paying attention to things like nuances in feelings or emotions. And eventually, the confession by my father to my mother—a lengthy period of intimacy outside their marriage—blindsided her, unhinged her. She never divorced him, and she never forgave him.

"I would love a gin and tonic," my father would have said on one of those summer days we were together, as he had settled into another perfect sunset after another perfect day of reading and sunning and birding and gardening and resting. And I would happily serve him, smile, and walk away from him to pull his expensive gin from the freezer, crack several cubes of ice from a tray to pile into the glass, nearly fill it to the brim with syrupy alcohol, a quarter inch from the top before a final splash of fancy tonic and lime. Always the same, his drink.

"*Thaannkk yoouu,*" he sang as I handed him the cocktail. He was rounding up his eighth decade then; he was a needy old man, a needy and lonely old man. I wanted him cared for, and for those couple of weeks it was simple: the beach, fresh fish, the piano, books, gin, wine, cigars, the channel outside the dining room window, the sunset. He had become softer, with tearing eyes, soupy-sad eyes or joyously-laughing-and-wetter-still eyes; tears that came from slowing breaths and gratitude kept slipping from his squinting corners and fell without notice to his chin. Even still, I kept my attention on his slippery-fish hands, his touches, and nudged my children out of his reach, held myself in front of him as proctor, as peacekeeper. I kept all of us safe.

For more than fifty years, we shared Jungle Beach. He was a preppy L.L. Bean swim trunks dad, and when I was younger and on the beach with him, I wore his Hanes boxers, extra-large, cotton plaids as a swimsuit. I admired my strong ballet legs poling through. I sunned myself on a blanket away from him; I studied the wind frilling the boxers, chilling my thighs, bumping gooses on my legs. And I watched him walk alone into the ocean and step into the crashing waves, the ripping currents. He braced the cold, with his skinny man legs supporting his six-foot awkward frame, allowing the salty hold to swallow him whole. He did not once turn around to see if we were watching him; he was, I thought, fully embraced by the sea. He was home. Some days back then he walked to the far end of Jungle, east, where the naked beach lay and where he often stayed, peeling off his swim trunks to bathe bare in the sun and ride himself clean in the ocean breakers.

Surviving him was my cross to bear, but his as well, and my mother's too. Because trauma is cellularly communal, biologically universal, trauma is a shared experience, literally and invisibly. It penetrates blood and bones just like music;

it infests the air we breathe and the words we speak. And the resulting variations of physical, emotional, or spiritual wounds linger and root within all of us, becoming our subsequent gestures, judgments, and behaviors alongside our passions, our brilliances, our curiosities and our fears. And then what? We pass them on, or we rub them off on one another.

Was my father a survivor of sexual molestation? I don't know. Did he have idiosyncratic sexual longings? My answer, yes. How come? The line between loving touch and inappropriate touch was never drawn by him and perhaps not ever for him. He was a child prodigy, a genius, raised by parents of the Greatest Generation. My parents were both taught that children were best seen and not heard. The world around them inspired frugality, building for their futures, following rules, and working hard for "the man." I'd imagine there would have been a lot of pent-up energy, bottled-up stress, stifled emotions, and tragically stuffed away desires.

I think it's common for children to replicate the templates of love and nurturance present in the environments they grew up in. What also appears common is a child's inability to objectively define or understand dysfunctional behavior enacted by their caretakers. And what also seems plausible is that when a child navigates trauma and becomes yoked to fear, over time the fear escalates, accelerates, and can expand into a destroyer of joy and light.

But is it possible that vulnerability as a result of trauma can be holy? Is it possible that a weakened heart in the aftermath of trauma can be revelatory, and damaged love can be revolutionary? Instead of succumbing to the ego's alliance with fear, what if our reactions to trauma were slowed and shape-shifted away from fear and we deferred instead to intuition and presence of spirit and prayer, and what if, by paying closer attention to the soul within, awe always won, held hands with suffering while remaining steadfast in its commitment to a higher vibration?

My father's life wound down in an assisted living facility in Minnesota. One of the nurses had notified our family that his time was approaching, and I took the last flight out of Cleveland and joined my nephew and my sister in the room where he lay ("his cell," he had called it). I'd hoped to tell him I loved him. I wanted to assure him of that. And while the three of us sat on the floor below where he lay motionless, barely breathing in bed, I suggested we open the large bottle of Scotch that was sitting next to the television set opposite him. "Let's toast him," I said with a small smile, and my nephew found us some glasses and we drank the entire bottle together, one shot at a time, and waited for him to die. After a few more hours, in a room with a bed and a window, a dresser, a chair and a nightstand, he drew in one final and gasping inhale. And he died. And we toasted him. And we told him we loved him.

The sun's dawning stirred the gulls as usual, prodded them into their delicate dance along the rooftop over my head, over me where I lay in bed in our family's home in Martha's Vineyard, the bed my father used to sleep in. It had been a year since his death.

I still pictured him in that bed, his feet facing south like mine, always on the right side when he shared it with my mother, on the left side when she stopped coming. On that day, the sliding glass door beyond the bed frame that led to the small deck outside was slightly open, and the wet mist and salted air settled on the sheets and the kantha blanket, all damp like the palms of my hands.

My father's urn and his cremated remains inside of it sat on the kitchen counter. I had placed it there the night before, my preparation to bring him to his grave. Stems of lilies and small branches of hydrangeas I had cut the day before and strung with twine and wrapped in wet towels suspending their lives a little longer lay quietly in my basket. The basket was set next to the urn. My father loved the varieties of hydrangeas: lacecap, mophead, mountain, and smooth; lavender, violet, magenta, and green. He had planted all of those varieties in the garden outside that kitchen. The fog was dense. If there had been fishermen departing the bay at that moment, I wouldn't have been able to see them. But I knew the water must've been calm because I did not hear the clanging bell of the buoy down the channel, unless it was just that the morning's fog had swallowed its *bong-bong* song whole. It was 6:00 a.m.

I poured a shot of Bulleit rye malt whiskey and toasted him one last time. I took a picture of the glass and thought, *This is for you and me, Pops*, lifting the glass. *Let's go.* His love for Jungle Beach was equal to mine; to be on its shoreline was to experience the soul's rest—the underworlds, the otherworlds, peace. I had driven over there the day before and chosen stones for his grave.

"Lavender is a good choice," Susan had told me. Susan was the cemetery's groundskeeper. She dug my father's grave the night before I brought him and had counseled me on what plantings would be good choices for the sand and clay earth I was burying my father in. It was farther east than Jungle, farther east than the nude beach; the plot sat north of South Road beyond two steep, curving hills but still close enough for the misty sea air to find him and mix its salt and foamy bubbles in within the deadened souls, speckle the decay.

"It won't require a lot of maintenance, especially since he's facing south." An elegant Japanese snowbell stood right in the middle and top end of his cemetery plot. "Bell-shaped flowers will drip in the springtime, fall onto him," Susan added.

I opened the heavy bag of him,
I balanced the dry pounds of him, the ash on my hands
and bone flecks and white chips and teeth,
and dust
and poured
him
(us)
into
the deep hole
like a sandbox.
He was piled ash below me.
I piled him.
I wondered what to do with the bag.

I dropped in seashells. I dropped in Jungle stones. The remains of him were paler (gray) than the rusty clay of the deep earth encasing him. I studied the two shades together, the island dirt, my father. "It does well in sandy soil," I remembered Susan saying about the lavender. "It will thrive without much care."

I closed my eyes after a long stare at him and then found the shovel Susan had left nearby and refilled my father's grave. I lay under the Japanese snowbell and fell asleep. The sun rose.

* Sandalwood oil: one cup water, two tablespoons vodka, five drops sandalwood essential oil, five drops of tea tree oil, five drops lemon essential oil.

The mattress she slept on was memory foam. Her bed frame was white oak, one of the most resistant, resilient woods in the furniture market. White oak, like my mother, had the ability to refuse to give in to dents, scratches—wear and tear. She and that bed were two of the only things that survived her house fire, which happened way back before she moved to Florida and before I moved her from Florida to Indiana but after she had kicked my father out of the house.

My mother was overtaken by scoliosis when she was fifteen; her graceful walk glitched, her balance faltered. Her tender spine quietly collapsed, turned, and bent her away from a promise of poise. She was meant to be a ballerina. She was meant for what so many young girls fancied: becoming a real-life fairy. But she ended up in a body-encasing cast through her teens, from her collarbone to her hip bones. And as she grew taller, the casts were replaced and grew in size along with her. Eventually, in her forties, way beyond her dreaming years, she underwent multiple surgeries and rehabilitated in more modern versions of body casts, sleek fiberglass with Velcro straps on the sides, like a life-sized, wearable coffin in white. The casts hung lifeless on hangers in her clothing closet, accumulated in the corner next to her luxurious gowns, silken blouses, cashmere cardigans, and linen suits. Her wardrobe was untailored, elastic waisted, and modern to accommodate and hide her less than perfect silhouette, and at the same time she mesmerized, became unmissable in billowing yet chic movie star ensembles. I spent hours in that closet playing, slipping into her casts like an exotic Frida Kahlo, donning imaginary blown-out floral headpieces, flipping woven skirts and wildly colorful shawls, ruby-red lips, charcoaled eyes.

"Let me see you," she called, hunched over her paper-work at her desk. "Come here." And I nervously hunted for shoes to pair with an outfit I had slipped into, the body cast caging me over the wild arrangements of her things I'd put together, hoping she would love it. I glided, floated, twirled toward her, I spun, dancing my way from her bedroom to the study where she sat at her desk. But she stayed bent and intent over her deskwork.

"Mom," I said to get her attention, and she briefly, side-ways, checked me out.

"Now hang it up," she said the next moment. "Put everything back exactly as you found it, all facing the right direction." The smell of her stayed with me afterward, her heavy sweet rose scent.

She had my back and my sisters' backs checked by a doctor every six months. "Bend over and touch your toes," he said, and I'd fold in half and pull my hands behind my ankles, tuck my head in between my knees. *Not a chance will mine twist like hers,* I thought to myself, and I prayed my spine would never collapse. Ever.

Without exception, every surgery and every grueling attempt at repairing her spine failed. The doctors couldn't unbend her; the steel supports were never enough.

In 1955, my twenty-three-year-old mother caught the attention of a young medical student in the hospital where she worked in New York City. She was whistling Bach's "Sleepers Wake" in the elevator standing next to him, a melody he knew better than she did. Destiny accompanied her whistle in his ear, shifted his focus, and caused him to notice not only the ease of the melody from her lips but also her impressive bosoms supporting the notes coming toward him. They coffee-klatched after that, met at nearby diners, learned they had other things in common: love of fine art, theater, dance, a lack of religious affiliation; she was an atheist, he an agnostic.

"He never actually proposed," she told me. But recalling the story, she said he'd proposed (too) early on in their dating period, so she'd turned him down. She wanted him to work a little harder for it. But then the idea just slipped away; he forgot all about it. "So, I went ahead, picked a date, and planned it myself."

I never heard her complain about her back, but sometimes I heard her suddenly gasp. At times, I heard her moan quietly when something shifted inside her body and jolted her from dull acceptance of her condition into a moment of unspeakable pain.

*Because of the bike accident, I began to experience mindful movement differently. Even though as I trained throughout my dance career I always believed I could learn something new each day and be constantly surprised by a changed understanding of my body's potential, the accident and its aftermath elevated my movement practice to a more heightened sacred experience of curiosity, a body prayer that unfolded moment by moment. After my accident, I became*

*aware of how my body intuited how it wished to move and how it was constantly responding to the space I was inhabiting. I felt my being was part of a higher vibration that enveloped everyone and everything. I had music on, but it was incidental to the shapes and rhythms my body initiated. And my movements were not only in relationship with the room I was inhabiting, but my movements time traveled as well, stirring up past experiences and memories or projecting into future realities. I relived the past through movement. I manifested the future, in movement.*

*Once working out in my basement, I had put my legs in a deep forward lunge, lowering my right shoulder until it was tucked behind my right knee where it became a fulcrum point. My shoulder being wedged there caused my spine to release, which in turn recruited my hip flexors to lengthen, igniting the electricity of the fascia at my low back, the web-like messaging circuitry. With my hands on the floor in front of me, I stretched my left leg off the floor behind me and then my right leg off the floor in front of me. It's a fairly well-known yoga pose; the Sanskrit name lurked somewhere in my past, but the name wasn't registering. Ultimately, I wasn't striving to accomplish predetermined goals with the shapes my body was forming; I was simply following a natural progression of my body's needs. Finally, I collapsed within the framework of that shape and was suddenly flayed open on my right shoulder and right side; I was an exact replica of how I had landed after my bike accident. The physical memory of that event came barreling back and I was reliving the trauma, but I was in my basement and not on a bike path. My body remembered and tensed but then moved through the physical trauma of the accident differently, with curiosity, with a chance to emotionally heal and physically reroute the experience. It was an unexpected and spontaneous rescue. It was life changing. Within days, it also triggered a reflection:*

*For decades I had succumbed to uncontrollable weeping after sexual intercourse. Every orgasm led to wet grief, an immediate corporeal and spiritual unwinding I was unable to control. It wasn't until intercourse transitioned into an act of procreation that my response changed and the mourning lessened, the tears subsided. Without realizing it, I had successfully rerouted the somatic and psychic experience of my past.*

*Once you start approaching your body with curiosity rather than with fear, everything shifts.*
—BESSEL VAN DER KOLK

I wanted my mother to sit and breathe mindfully, and I said I would do it with her. I wanted her to breathe intentionally through her atrophied limbs; she was reducing in size, exponentially. "Expand, Mama," I said, wishing somehow she could connect herself back to her past, to her painful memories, and reconfigure their impact, find awe, find holy, find love.

She had purged, whittled her collections of collections down until only a handful of shells remained. And delicate beads and rare combs. She had held on to her massive book of Shakespeare's works and her one plant—an *Oxalis triangularis*, whose leaves folded in at night and resembled butterflies resting until the next day's light when wings reopened and fluttered. She kept special pillows and hats, purses, linens, shoes, bracelets, rings, photographs, literature. Music was everything; Bach was everything.

Approximately one heartbeat before COVID-19 overwhelmed the world, we moved her into an assisted living facility where she had to give up the two things she coveted most: her privacy and her independence. She may have blamed me for that, she must have, although she never said so. But once I had eyes on her every day, things changed. I saw how tricky she had been disguising her infirmities, hiding her absentmindedness, her weird diet, her accidents, her distortions of truth. Living alone she had built a beautiful, illusive reality. I befriended her. I gave her my heart and cared for her.

I showed up daily. Cleaned, bookkept, laundered, dog walked, grocery shopped, organized meds, paid bills. I felt since I had orchestrated her departure from a life of independence, I owed her. I also believed that eventually she would tell me how sorry she was, she would tell me how she should have intercepted my father's hands all those years ago. What I realized, too late, was that I had perpetuated her story by becoming part of the secret; I was complicit. She knew I could have challenged her but I didn't, and she also knew I loved her deeply despite what she hadn't done, and she knew that I fiercely believed in love, even our love.

In bed, she gathered pillows around her, under an armpit, stacked behind her shoulders, and thousands more supported her head, her hips and elbows, all of her sharp places.

I bathed her, held the Dial soap against her neck and across her shoulders. I stroked the high right side of her back and followed it to the lower valley across and over her spine. My lathering hand slid down to her left rib cage. I soaped her armpits and kneeled to clean under her feet and in between her toes. I held and helped her as she rose from the plastic chair. She hugged me all wet. I balanced her, and as I held the bath towel in front of her, she folded into it and into me.

She had lots of her bits laid out on a side table next to her bed: medicines, tissues, cough drops, nail clipper, phone charger, and index cards; she scribbled notes in boxy uppercase handwriting. I saved them.

Strands of her wiry gray hair floated everywhere, stuck onto everything, came home with me. And at one point she bought herself a gray wig, a smooth and full bob with a flip, but I never saw her wear it. It lived on top of her Tiffany lampshade, on her dresser next to the dish of seashells and sand dollars. Her backside faced that side table most days, curled on itself sometimes all day long, a shuttered bug. Her *New Yorkers* slid around her on the bed, disappeared under her fleece throws, disappeared just like everything else had disappeared because she was certain her black cardigan had been stolen, her bronze Buddha had been stolen, her cargo pants had been stolen, her coffee packets, her magazines, her tissues, her tramadol.

"Those pants you just bought me—they're missing," she said, disgusted. "I'm not moving from my seat (her sofa) until they put a lock on my closet door," she announced one day.

"You're going to sleep all night on the sofa you mean? You're going on strike?" I smiled as I asked.

And her jowl dropped a little lower. Her fish mouth drooped. "I am not moving until I get a lock. Everything will be stolen unless it's locked up." And then she smiled too. She was becoming funny and goofy in a way that made me wonder if maybe I'd been too busy protecting myself from her and being angry with her that I missed those funny parts; maybe I never really saw her because I was struggling so much with my story. She was very brave. During that final year especially when her world dwindled down to only her sofa and the struggles of lowering herself to it and the struggles of lifting herself up again.

In bed, her swollen feet stayed crossed over each other. A couple of her toes had been removed long ago, a solution to neuropathic pain. Her arches had fallen, her toenails thickened crookedly, and when standing, she barely balanced on her slabs of dead tissue; her feet were useless.

"I just love her. We make an unusual and funny pair," she confided to me one day about Joan, a fellow resident she met in the lobby of her facility. My mom at that time was using her motor scooter to travel the interior of the facility, and she met Joan. Tango, Mom's poodle, trotted alongside her as she navigated the hallways and gripped Tango's leash. COVID, in that way, had been a blessing for my mom. The dog walkers were not allowed in the building (nor was I), but if she delivered her dog to the front door, a touchless hand-off was allowed. Joan became her confidant, a storyteller, a co-conspiring make-believer who also lived in a tiny corner of reality, who had items stolen from her, who wandered internally but made it a point to be in the lobby whenever my mom was there waiting for her dog to be returned to her from its walk.

My mother was held together with bolts and screws. She needed her Velcro strapping shoes to hold her deadly feet steady, to create a more solid foundation for her bones to stack over; she willed functionality into the process of move-ment. Moment by moment as though compelled toward an Emerald City and with the stylized gait of a Tin Man all dried up, she forged ahead courageously, from a kitchen to a sofa, from a toilet to a bed, from a bed to a walker, bracing the handles with a mountain of knuckles, connected to a hardened twisted spine, inside out and in again, her coiling bitter vertebrae, a sadly jaded and beautiful human, childlike, tender, broken-hearted. My mother never said she was afraid when she walked, but she must have been. I was.

My mother, along with thirteen other residents where she lived, tested positive for COVID ten days shy of her vaccination appointment, one year to the day from when I had moved her from Florida to Indiana. For the first couple of days after her diagnosis, she was practically asymptomatic. "Only tired," she said. That was all, like she had a cold. But on the third day, she couldn't breathe.

*how do you feel when you think of others as light?*

Well, when I was growing up, I didn't default to thinking of others as light. But I did think of myself as light, like a sun, like a candle's flame.
I was alive.
I was a miracle.
I was light.
But that wasn't really it, *was* it?
I was supposed to figure out that *you* were light, as well.

"Hello, Tuni," the voicemail began, "I don't like to leave messages like this, but your mother is going to the hospital. Her oxygen level dropped, and she is having difficulty breathi—"
    I screamed.
    I dialed the facility where my mother lived (*fuck* COVID) and ran for the keys to my car. "Good evening, Anthology of Meridian Hills. This is Mary speaking." I floored it. I was eleven blocks away.

"Mary!" I screamed into the phone. "Is she there? This is Tuni. Is she there? Is she there? Is the ambulance . . . ?" My throat was closing; my eye sockets were swelling.

"Oh . . . Tuni," she whispered back, "she's in there. They closed the door. They're in their seats."

"Can you stop them, Mary?" I was screaming. "Please! Can you tell them I'm almost there? I'm one minute away; please, please don't let them drive away."

"I can't leave my . . ." Mary tried to explain.

"I'm almost—I'm here! I'm here! I can see the truck!" and I felt my heart seams burst, my skull crack.

"God bless," Mary whispered.

I hockey-stopped my Jeep in front of the ambulance, grabbed a mask.

"I'm her daughter." I ran to the EMT's window. "Can I see her? Can I see her and tell her I love her?" I folded my hands together in the shape of prayer. The sky was falling.

The EMT looked directly into my eyes from inside the ambulance, and then she slowly opened the driver side door toward me. Her eyes bored holy light into mine. "Tell me her name," she said calmly, and I told her. "Be very quick," she added, and pulled me with her toward the back of the ambulance and opened the back doors.

Her gray hair was painted black on her skull; her sunken cheeks all but disappeared under the hardened ridges of her cheekbones. Her nose and mouth hid underneath the moisture of an oxygen mask and her eyes were yo-yos, like an optical illusion of black-and-white striping spirals, spinning, spinning, spinning. Her black-inked saucer's eyes were drilling and spilling fear. Those were not my mother's eyes.

"Mama!" I screamed at her, wanting to pull her back, "Mama, I love you." I flailed and reached for her. "You will get stronger, Mama. They will help you! I love you, Mama!"

The EMT nodded toward the door. "We need to take her," she said, closing the first one, closing the second one.

"Thank you," crumbled out of my mouth.

"We will take good care of her; she needs our help." The EMT pulled her driver's door closed. I watched them slowly wind around my Jeep. My stomach seized. There was no siren, just a quiet spinning red light. My stomach seized again, docked into dire. *It won't take her,* I thought, or prayed—*What did it matter what it was called?* —I wanted to ride next to her, hold her to life. And since the emergency room staff thought she was dying, after I'd checked in, and proved daughtership, revealing primarily a child's hysteria, they discarded ER protocol and allowed me into her room. I crept in. She was laid out ghostly white, encased in sterile linens, tubes, drips. Rhythms of mechanical air pulsed in, pulled out, whooshing, beeping, red lights blinking. I focused on the small rises and falls of her chest. *Are you alive, are you alive, are you alive?* I thought, or prayed. She was a statue in state, frozen in motion, gesturing hands in stone at her sides, rings and bracelets, thousands of them hovering around her withering arms. Her watch.

That "We think she is dying" declaration was the third time in two weeks I'd been told that her time had come. I'd been invited into her emergency room to stand by, stand watch, witness, process her holy departure. COVID was ridiculing her. The woman who micromanaged her body's pounds and ounces, who finessed her public image at every turn or tumble, was leaching out, transitioning into iron and manganese and zinc and chromium and nickel; drenched in fentanyl, she was unresponsive, colorless, and flat tongued.

The TV above flashed HGTV, and then after I wiggled the remote, the History channel, Nickelodeon, Hallmark, distractions for a dying patient. She remembered and began humming Bach, as though bent over her sleek beechwood desk, managing her inherited properties, yellow pencil in hand, tracking numbers, humming to her confidant, her soul mate soother. It wasn't the first time I thought she was tapping out, racing with Bach toward the finishing line.

The nurse wrapped flesh-colored tape around the opiate syringe dancing in her deteriorating flesh and bone, and in tempo, kept flicking the needle. The tape added a healthy tone to my mother's arm, an illusion of good health.

Daisy was *unremembering*.

She *unremembered* when the blankets became too heavy and itchy, failed to remember how she threw them off desperately, exposing her soft rounded belly, her sideways lodged rib cage and grossly swollen shoulder joint, her breasts long and flat, like canoes.

She *unremembered* the quivering she experienced, the chill, until she begged for those same blankets back again, the ones she had moments before thrown off and had to be re-draped and re-swaddled, the nurse tucking them in all the way around her ears and chin, across her forehead and under her torso, her bum, consuming her consumed body; she was a muslin shrine. She was desert heat and slipping memories of *Sea Cloud* and travel, Moroccan tombs, sacred mosques, jewels, textiles, luxurious gifts and souvenirs mantled, pedestaled above love. She murmured incoherently exotic dreamings, quickly *unremembering* the physical world. She glitched and liquid exhaled—an attack of uncontrollable coughing. She plowed the warm coverings off again. Bent her bowed knees and kneecaps up toward freedom. She hooked the bed's bar on her left with her frail bony fingers, oversized knuckles, and tipped her torso portside, holding.

"What are you doing, Mama? Mama! Where are you going? Mama?" And murky waste receded from her. Her tightly held dignity and pride spilled, soiled and soaked her bedding. "Mama." I stood and stroked her tired, broken spine. Her fingers released the bar and she recoiled, loosened the post after her surrender.

"Do we need to change your bedding, dear?" Another nurse arrived and saw the sewage.

"No," was what she managed to say. And they cleansed her quietly while she remained on her side, with eyes pinched shut, on a sea cloud.

I stayed with and beside her, cold in her room for an infinity of hours, the relentless beeping, the monitoring of everything except the essence of her. She was re-tidied, re-medicated, readmitted. They mummy-wrapped her again, swaddled her in a putrid cocktail of medicine crack and loose, foul, shit mix.

She didn't die from COVID, at least not in the obvious sense, not how millions of others died outright, within days of contracting it. Hers was a painstaking, lung-rattling, breath-cinching eleven-month slog. A few weeks after the last ER visit, I was with her, back at her apartment. She had completed a long stint at a rehabilitation center, more nightmarish for her than the hospital; she said it was like a prison cell equipped with a bedside commode and intermittent therapies she washed down with thickened (therapeutic) water. She was grateful to be back in her room, with her beautiful things around her and the classical music filling her.

But her lungs gave out, again. And back at the hospital she went, again. And they wanted to intubate her, again. And they asked if she had a DNR or a living will, again. And I listed off her medications from memory to the nurses (which was no small feat) and contacted family members, again. (Was this the time she would finish the race once and for all, cross over and leave me in her wake?) And as many times as she had reminded me that she wanted to die alone, by herself in a room with no one with her, I was there next to her, defying her wishes. I owed her. Deep down, she was unresolved, and I thought I could at least fucking hold her hand.

I lay next to her on the rubber-and-plastic hospital mattress; I snailed into her backside, just as I had done as a little girl. I craved her. It wasn't me showing up for her, I knew that. It was me wanting her to show up for me. It was still me wanting her to say she was sorry, that was all. How was it possible that I still wanted this from her, that I still wanted my dying mother to repent?

Her once lively and magnificent breasts were deflated, emptied of nurturance. Her rheumatic hands were spotted redundantly with age, which she despised and for which she still had me purchasing spot removal, age-eliminating products. Her arms were bruised and blackened from prods and punctures, injections in, fluids out, and her stoic face sweating and drenched, fit snug as a bug in the steroid-infused oxygen mask, the machine that pushed over and over again breaths we shared. *Could we heal together, Mama?*

Then days later, she came back to me and the world around her; she rebounded and reinflated. Humphrey Bogart and Peter Lorre acted on the hospital TV above her, *The Maltese Falcon.* She knew every actor, their black-and-white lips and old-fashioned mouths pursing, pressing, shaping polite and veiled dialogue cooing out of the remote lodged between her pillow-light atrophied thighs. "Sydney Greenstreet," she muttered and wept. *Her beauty, her beauty, her beauty,* I thought, watching as she wept and the film carried on.

She moved into a different assisted living facility only a few more minutes away from my home. We hired 24/7 home health care. She was terribly frail, exponentially weaker. Her red motor scooter sat quietly in her front storage closet; dozens of cannulas hung from its handlebars. The oxygen compressor stayed out in her living room; she needed oxygen at all times. Gone were the days of scooting along like a wild old braless hippie, *Top Gun* aviators, unbuttoned peasant blouse rippling as she rode.

She used to cook. Chicken meatballs with tarragon and whipped-up mushrooms in a toasted Wonder Bread cup. "What are you making?" I'd ask, watching her stir a big mishmash on the gas stove.

"*Gemish*," she said, a mélange of whatever was in the fridge, that was often what was for dinner: some type of ground meat, leftover rice, and raisins. Other Yiddish words sing-songed in and out of our kitchen, including: *Schmata*, a rag. *Baleboste*, a good homemaker. *Bissel*, a little bit. *Schlemiel*, clumsy. *Shlimazel*, bad luck. When the *schlemiel* spilled his soup, he probably spilled it on the *shlimazel*. *Noshing*, picking up little pieces for yourself. Noshing. (I am 100 percent noshing if I don't credit: https://www.dailywritingtips.com/the-yiddish-handbook-40-words-you-should-know/.)

My Bubele often told me I was *a gute neshome*, a good soul, and I loved when she said that; I believed her.

*Shalom*, deep peace.

*Shalom*. May deep peace be our miracle.

Her living footprint was halved yet again, her belongings were further divvied up or tossed away, her last apartment was much smaller, she was much smaller, the same as watching the candle get low, the flame diminishing, harder to see, harder to speak, harder to swallow. She held on to her can't-let-go-of's: her *Joy*, Jean Patou's elegant and no-longer-produced perfume. Several delicate and almost empty beveled glass vials of it were tucked artistically away on a shelf in her bathroom, but she swore to me up and down she never ever actually wore perfume under her earlobes, at her wrists, or on the nape of her neck; she just "happened" to smell that way, like tuberose, ylang-ylang blossom, and mouthwatering pear. Special editions of *Dance* magazines that featured her favorite ballerinas on its pages (or a photograph of me on the back cover) stayed stacked on her bookcase, the most unique Buddhas above those, the rarest beads of glass or

wood or bamboo above them. Rings—gold and silver—
encircled most of her fingers, and bangles piled high onto
her forearms, like a gypsy's.

"Thank you, my angel," she said, settling her sweet old
eyes on mine. "Thank you for helping me." Her gaze lifted,
and she suddenly laughed and repeated, "My angel." She
listened to Chopin. "He is so challenging to play, so complicated." She was drifting, fidgeting, pulling gently on her
shirt and mused, "She used to play Chopin, but she shouldn't
have." She was talking about Bubby. "She struggled; she
played him struggling. It was too much for her." And her
fidgeting escalated. "I sat on the stairway, you remember?
The stairs that overlooked the piano, you remember?"

"Yes, Mama, I remember," I said.

"I sat and listened to her," my mom continued, "I
watched her serious face—she was so determined."

"Did she know you were there, listening?" I asked her.

"Oh, of course, she knew." Her shoulder pinched forward into a shrug, and she continued, "Oh, Mama, you are
wonderful, applause, applause," and she rolled her eyes and
smiled. "That's what I told her, of course. That's what she
wanted me to say."

"That's sweet, you said that to her," I said.

But my mother's eyes narrowed. "She looked at me
when she finished," she said. "She eyed me over her sheet
music; she wanted me to say that, to tell her she was grand,"
she continued. "She shouldn't have played Chopin, not at
all. It was too advanced for her."

*She loved you*, I didn't think to say to my mother. *She is
love, you are love, we can all do this, we are all the same*, I
wanted so badly for my mother to see, the: *us. Unbury her*, I
prayed. *Be awed by her struggle, her vulnerabilities; love her.*

The white oak bed frame made it almost all the way to the
end, with its four slender posts and three iron birds topping

the posts (one had broken off in a move and then lived in a basket on her dresser, for safekeeping). But finally the white oak framed bed was replaced with a hospital bed, almost the cruelest backhand slam by COVID. My mother had fought way past logic in regards to keeping her beloved four-poster; I hated having to replace it. She loved her sleep—she bragged about what a good sleeper she was—and she loved it all the more because of her sturdy, resilient, resistant, courageous bed.

*Say amen. Say amend. Say yes. Say yes anyway.*
—OCEAN VUONG

I sat in my bathroom and waited for the scalding hot water
to cool enough for me to step into. I could have been folding
laundry or feeding my dogs, wiping down a shelf with the
cuff of my robe. I could have unloaded and loaded a dish-
washer because the water was that hot, and still I would have
had enough time to sit down and wait longer. But I didn't do
anything. I only sat in a chair, next to the tub, and waited. I
tilted my head at grief in the mirror and reflexively turned
my middle-aged dimpled body on an angle to thin it out,
and then I let it go, forgiving it. *Fish*, I thought, stepping in.

My skin reddened underneath the water's surface. I
grabbed the bar of soap and razor from the chair and began
the same lathering, her same strokes, the ritual I had memorized fifty years before. My calf drooped after the blade
pressed the flesh and left it behind. My left hand propped it
at the ankle; the right one imagined her heavier silver shaver
and the way she divided the thick foam along her shin. She
did not know how much I loved watching her bathe.

I placed my head under the water while plugging my
ears and leaving my nostrils out for air. I pulled up the
drain. With my eyes closed and ears still covered, I was a
racing fish, following the jets of a waterway; I was on top of

the current, flying. I was returning home upstream along a thunderous, cascading, rushing destiny. Life and death in a bathtub, Mama. "Mama," I said out loud while underwater, and then thought to myself, *Our layers of sadness need fresh air*. I have unearthed the mutations of our memories in order for us to be cleansed, to heal together. Trauma in my hands, I thought, could be reshaped into beauty, and with my hands over my ears and my eyes closed, I swam.

When I stood at my father's deathbed, my knees and thighs pressing against the rails of his bed, I watched the water drip from the dangling IV bag. I watched his respirations come and go, pause unpredictably, and then wildly catch, rattle, quicken, hover, and finally stop. I mourned and grieved, detached. And when I poured his ashes into the ground that following summer, deep into the vineyard clay, I had hoped he was relieved and unburdened. I'd hoped he'd found peace.

I was not with my mother the moment she passed away, which was exactly what she wanted (it was written in her will). In fact, carelessly and heartlessly, her caregiver texted me simply that on arrival to my mother's apartment, she was not able to locate her pulse. "Your mother passed," she texted. I heard news of my mother's death in a fourteen-word-long text.

I drank the following week away. I never suspected her story was going to end when it did. There were so many other times I had stood at her bedside in the hospitals preparing myself for the inevitability, but not that morning. That morning, I was "on my way," "just getting my coffee." That morning I was too late.

Just after she died, there she was in my dreams, a blackened smoke-filled tornado that spun and rooted at the

doorway of my childhood bedroom, twisting and destroy-
ing everything in its path. I was my mother's deferred dream
and her husband's child mistress. She never forgave me that.

But her coyish smile betrayed her, her careful laugh com-
miserated with me, her towering transparent opinions, her
refined manner, her pain, all of her bits she pressed deeply
into my skin and bones. We are colored the *same*; Mama,
we are the *yes*.

*If you are irritated by every rub,*
*how will you be polished?*

—*RUMI*

I am a guardian.
I am a nurse.
I am an aunt.
I am love.
I am allowed.
I am open.
I am comfort.
I am strong.
I ravish.
I trust.
I applaud. I applaud. I applaud.
I am rhythm.
I am a moving tiger.
I am a wild snake.
I am a fish.
I am the wind.
At death's door,
I am our pendulum, our dance.
The child in me sees the child in you.

When I was fourteen, I performed the role of Jasmine in the Children's Theatre Company's production of *Aladdin*. I wanted to quit the school during that time period, but I'd been taught that one should never quit what one starts. After the school year was over, I never again returned to that school or its main stage. But during that year—after *Aladdin*'s run—I was cast in *The Little Match Girl*, and in the spring, I was given a lead role in an original production entitled *Circle Is the Sun*, a collaboration between the artistic director, the faculty of the school, and us children. During the audition process of *Circle*, we were asked to compose lyrics and a melody, and within the following hours, we were called up to the stage one at a time to perform whatever we had come up with. I sang,

She's growing up fast. . . . . . . . . . G, C, C, C, C,
and left behind few. . . . . . . . . . . C, B-flat, C, B-flat, B-flat
She's loved, cried, sung a song . . . G, C, C, D, D, C
and learned to use the moods
   of the moon. . . . . . . . . . . . . . . .C, G, G, G, G, G, G, G, C
Mother, dreams are free. . . . . . . E, C, B-flat, B-flat, B-flat

*She's at the bay window overlooking the sea.*
*She marvels at the egrets, the ospreys, alone.*
*I can smell her, the tuberose, the ylang-ylang blossom,*
*the mouthwatering pear.*

# *epilogue*

I had the unique reward of truly befriending my mother during her last two spins around the sun, during her sacred unwind. It began when we moved her from Florida to Indiana, just before the pandemic settled in.

Long ago, when I was very young and living in Minnesota, I thought the name of the state "Indiana" was really funny because my mom's given name was Diana. Back then, I decided she should live there, in "In-Diana." How strange that it was the last place she lived.

In Indiana, she had recreated the beautiful home I grew up in, the surroundings of my youth that led to my creating and exploring and fashioning survival. The combs, the shells, the corals, her plants, her books, her Buddhas became my living and breathing dioramas of escape. Her curiosities colored my world of movement, her style influenced my dance language, and her struggles taught me to wonder about her pain, to wonder about someone else's suffering.

Her interests, her musings filled her with rapture, and rapture became my goal. And her jealousies and private competitions with me taught me self-reliance and independence and independence and fortitude. And her obsession with beauty without seeing or claiming her own inspired my thinking that there was beauty at every turn, and I saw it in everything along my way, day after day, in the cut downs, the takeovers, the bullyings and two-faces, the diminishings and disbelievings, the denials and shamings and blamings, desertions and cruelest of name-callings—beauty, no matter the depths of my despair, no matter the depths of her despair, I believed in beauty.

I visited my mother hours before she died. She was reclined on her bed. It was winter. It was the afternoon. The bedroom lights were off. Pillows bolstered and cushioned and surrounded her. It was impossible for her to lie down without them wedging every inch of her. She longed only for comfort and ease. Thanksgiving was in five days, and she told me she had picked out her outfit for our dinner. Her favorite caregiver was going to come with her. She was looking forward to visiting with all of my children, sharing a home-cooked meal with all of us.

I thought back to when I used to lie on her belly. Her sewing finished, she would have been reading a book by then, or a magazine. She would have propped it onto my back so I could lie on her and she could read. My father next to us on his side of the bed—he would have also been reading at that point. The deep thrumping and drumming of her heart replaced everything, churned me and my rhythms fully into hers, slowed my breaths, brought calm. The rumbles of her—her borborygmi. It was a word my father had used once playing the board game called Probe, a game similar to Hangman, where you guessed each other's words one letter at a time. Dr. Dad thought he was hilarious by choosing that word, a word only he could know—it was a medical term. I would have been nine or ten at the time, my sister two years older, but I was captivated by it the minute he pronounced it. Borborygmi was the grumbling tumbling you heard if your ear was pressed to another's belly— thrashing comings and goings and tumultuous depths of my mother's ocean, its deepest pulse, her heartbeat, the source of the sea, borborygmi. She had saved me without using her words, without confronting her husband, without endangering herself. Back then, I had thought I'd saved myself. But back then I hadn't noticed the hint he gave me when playing that game. He knew where my salvation lay. And back then she knew she was pulling me to safety, underwater daughter, she taught her. He knew where I could find solace, and so did she. When I visited her on that day before she died, standing next to her, I imagined us, the three of us together again, riding a grand and iron-framed bed.

I saw ancient turtles plunging
and mighty whales breaching
and fleeing krill and gulls and mergansers and pipers
in a harmony of currents and thrashing waves and the winds
like a wild blessing or an ancient secret.
And we glimpsed compassion
yes,
and forgiveness
yes,
and mercy at sea.

# acknowledgments

Please allow me to mention and thank:

Every single dance instructor/coach/colleague/director & student that crossed my path. I would never have accumulated the body wisdom that I inhabit, if not for all of you.

Technically, my story would have gone nowhere fast without my editor Jodi Fodor, who paid as close attention to my words as I did, and then upped me one, two and a million. I am endlessly grateful, JF.

Debra Engle, my mentor, and the embodiment of love
Amy Ferris, truth serum
David Kirkpatrick & The Story Summit
My bestie for life, Angela Gordon
Steven Rydberg, for the cover, I am still pinching myself—forever, thank you
Linda Schreyer & her Slipper Camps

Inspirations Lidia Yuknavitch & Ocean Vuong
Dr. Katie Peck, who put me back together again
Brooke Warner for saying yes
Shannon Green, for assembling, reiterating, clarifying, fixing,
& tying together all the things, perfectly
Melissa Hunt, the one who pushed me into Brooke's yes
CIM party life
Stacy Marinelli
Beth Furlong
Sharon Bialy
Martha and her sisters
Akasha & Jennifer Ewert & our crew
Rock Candy Photography
Kaleb Talarico
Music, music, music . . . all music, all the time
kathy
J
B
J
Heartmates, soul mates T, O, M, J, L, & J

# playlists for
## *Underwater Daughter*

Apple Music

Spotify

# about the author

ANTONIA DEIGNAN is the mother of five grown children—three young men and two young women. But years before the adventure of motherhood, she parlayed her childhood years of theater into a professional ballet and jazz dance career. Following a bike accident at fifty-five, which temporarily eliminated movement from her daily existence, she found new expression through writing. The years of recovery after the accident became a gift. She rediscovered and ultimately found sanctuary in processing survival of childhood trauma through her body's art and her mind's dreams. One thing she has learned through writing her memoir is this: her most favorite thing is moving alongside the rhythms within her; it is her soul's calling. To move is to connect with the rest of the world. She has multiple publications in magazine and online formats, and this is her first book.

You can find more resources and information about Antonia at www.antoniadeignan.com.

*Author photo © Rock Candy Photo*

# selected titles from she writes press

She Writes Press is an independent publishing company founded to serve women writers everywhere. Visit us at www.shewritespress.com.

*Poetic License: A Memoir* by Gretchen Eberhart Cherington. $16.95, 978-1-63152-711-1. At age forty, with two growing children and a consulting company she'd recently founded, Gretchen Cherington, daughter of Pulitzer Prize–winning poet Richard Eberhart, faced a dilemma: Should she continue to silence her own voice? Or was it time to speak her truth—even the unbearable truth that her generous and kind father had sexually violated her?

*The Sergeant's Daughter: A Memoir* by Teressa Shelton. $16.95, 978-1-63152-721-0. Every night of her childhood life, Teressa's sergeant father brings his military life home, meeting each of his daughters' infractions with extreme punishment for them all. At first cowed by her father's abuse and desperate to believe that maybe, one day, things will change, Teressa ultimately grows into a young woman who understands that if she wants a better life, she'll have to build it for herself—so she does.

*Fourteen: A Daughter's Memoir of Adventure, Sailing, and Survival* by Leslie Johansen Nack. $16.95, 978-1-63152-941-2. A coming-of-age adventure story about a young girl who comes into her own power, fights back against abuse, becomes an accomplished sailor, and falls in love with the ocean and the natural world.

*Being Mean: A Memoir of Sexual Abuse and Survival* by Patricia Eagle. $16.95, 978-1-63152-519-3. Patricia is thirteen when her sexual relationship with her father, which began at age four, finally ends. As a young woman she dreams of love but it's not until later in life that she's able to find the strength to see what was before unseeable, rise above her shame and depression, and speak the unspeakable to help herself and others.

*Fortunate Daughter: A Memoir of Reconciliation* by Rosie McMahan. $16.95, 978-1-64742-024-6. Intimate, unsentimental, and inspiring, this memoir explores the journey of one woman from abused little girl to healed adult, even as she maintains her relationship with her former abuser.

*Now I Can See The Moon: A Story of a Social Panic, False Memories, and a Life Cut Short* by Alice Tallmadge. $16.95, 978-1-63152-330-4. A first-person account from inside the bizarre and life-shattering social panic over child sex abuse that swept through the US in the 1980s—and affected Alice Tallmadge's family in a personal, devastating way.